presents:

MY First BILINGUAL Workbook

Mi Primer Cuaderno Bilingüe

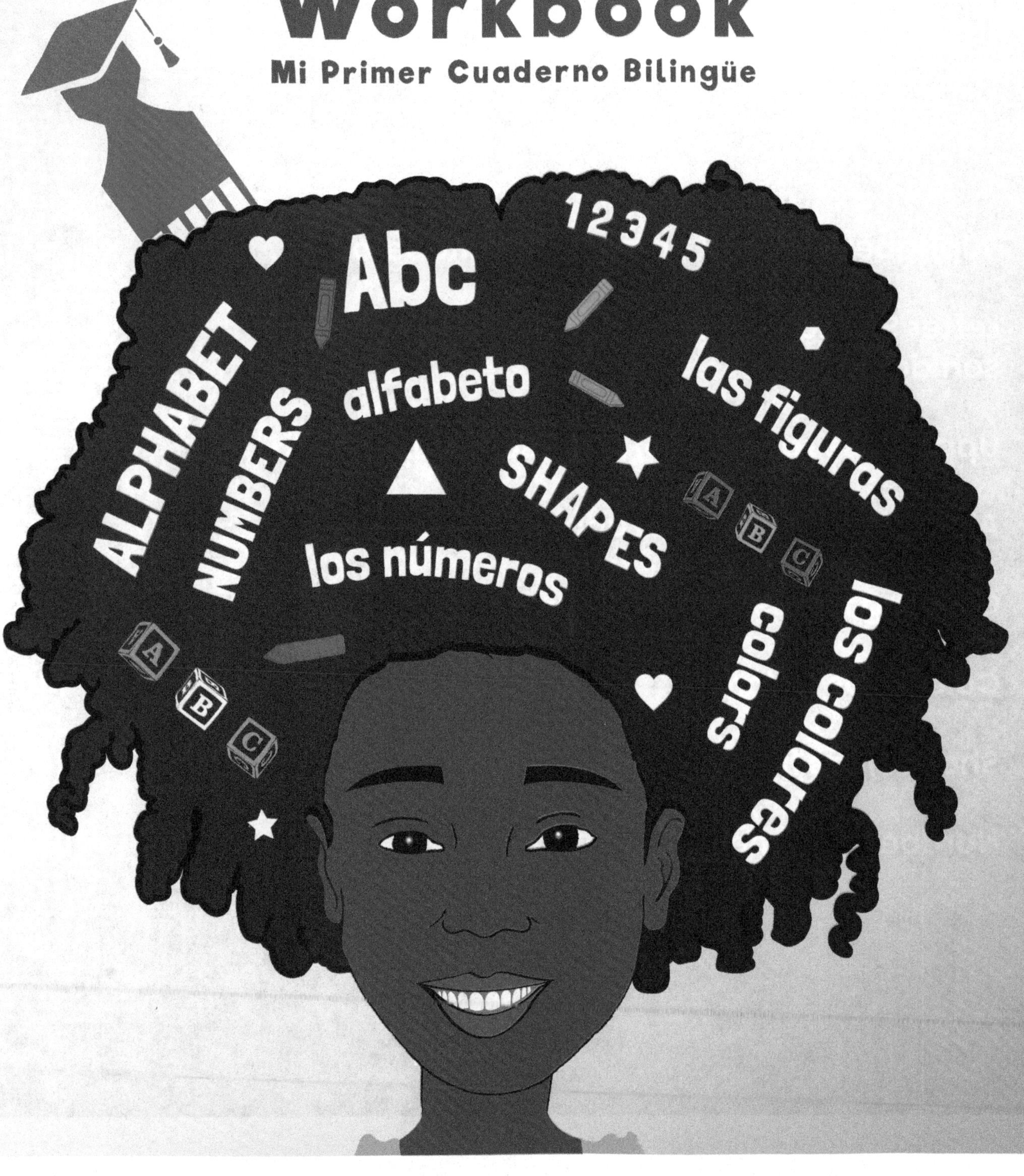

Abc

12345

ALPHABET

NUMBERS

alfabeto

SHAPES

las figuras

los números

colors

los colores

Table of Content

The Bigger the Fro the More I know

Practice writing the English Alphabet

A B C D E F G

H I J K L M

N O P Q R S T

U V W X Y Z

The Bigger the Fro the More I know

Practice writing the Spanish Alphabet

A B C CH D E F

G H I J K L LL M

N Ñ O P Q R RR S

T U V W X Y Z

Name: ____________________ Date: ______________

Directions: Trace each letter. Then write it on your own below.

Instrucciones: Traza cada letra. Luego escríbalo abajo.

Uppercase

A

A A A A

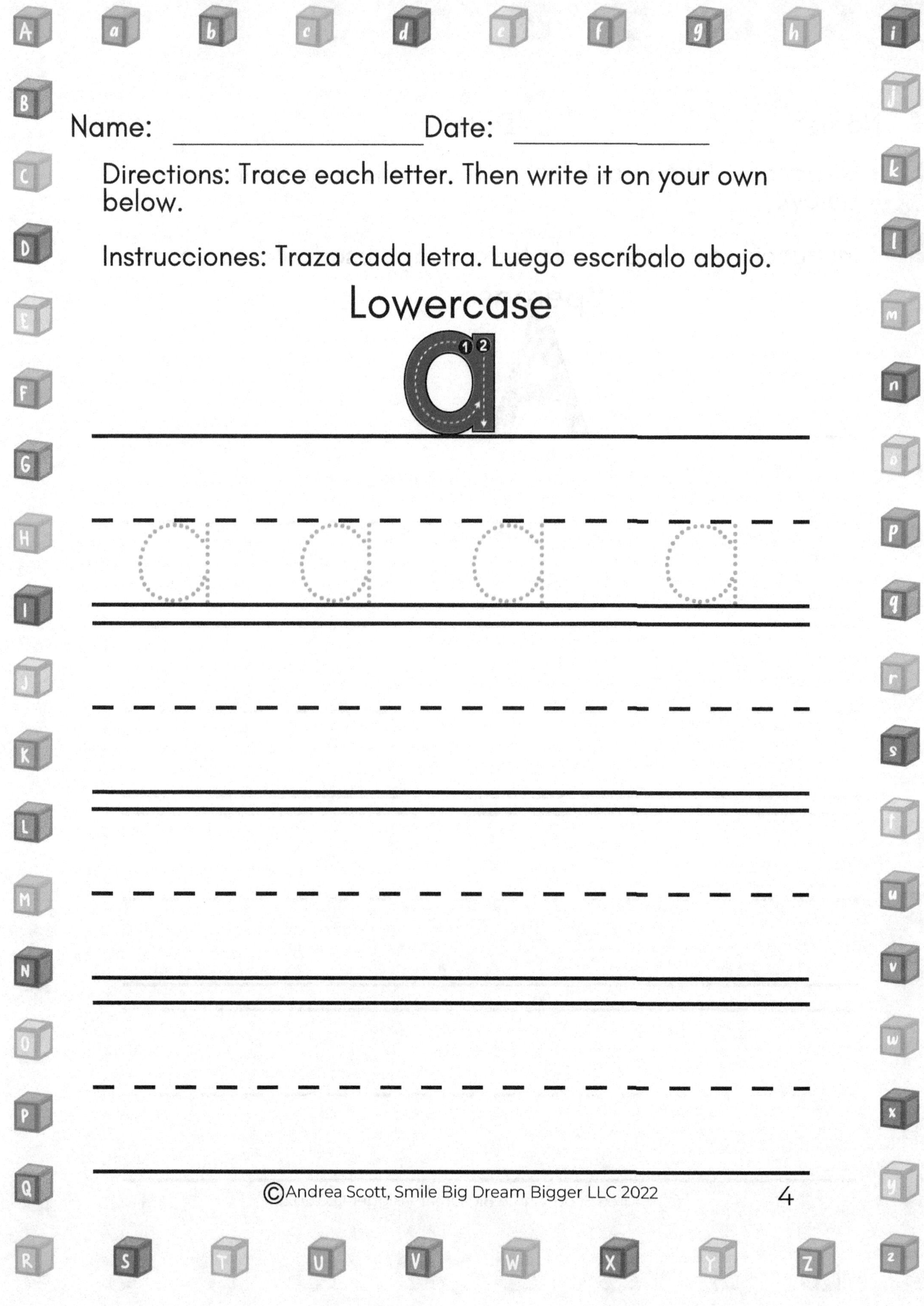

Name: ____________________ Date: ________________

Directions: Trace each letter. Then write it on your own below.

Instrucciones: Traza cada letra. Luego escríbalo abajo.

Lowercase

Name: ____________________ Date: ______________

Directions: Trace each letter. Then write it on your own below.

Instructions: Traza cada letra. Luego escríbalo abajo.

Uppercase B

B B B B

Name: ____________________ Date: ______________

Directions: Trace each letter. Then write it on your own below.

Instrucciones: Traza cada letra. Luego escríbalo abajo.

Lowercase b

Name: ____________________ Date: ______________

Directions: Trace each letter. Then write it on your own below.

Instrucciones: Traza cada letra. Luego escríbalo abajo.

Uppercase C

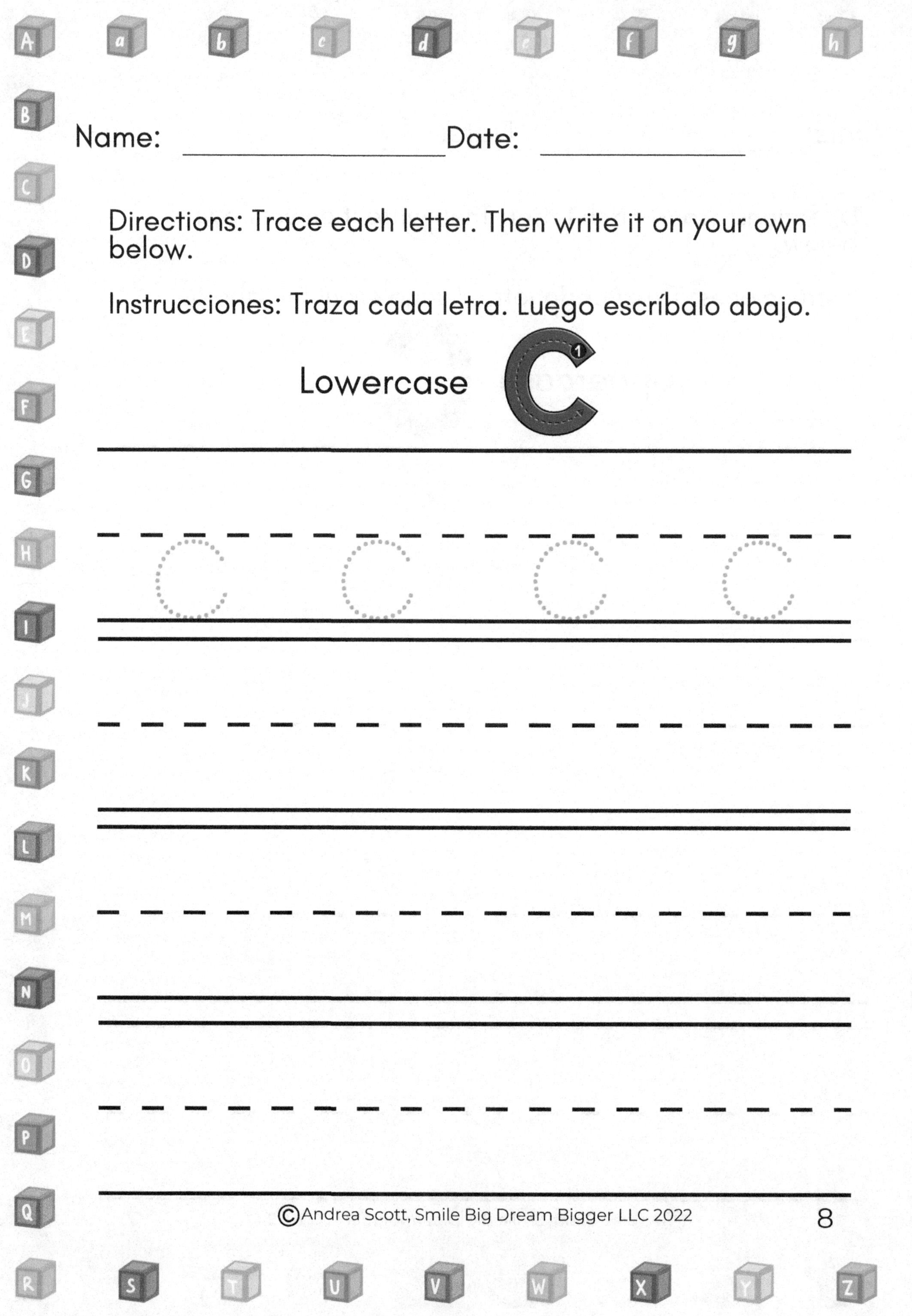

Name: ____________________ Date: ______________

Directions: Trace each letter. Then write it on your own below.

Instrucciones: Traza cada letra. Luego escríbalo abajo.

Lowercase c

Name: ____________________ Date: ______________

Directions: Trace each letter. Then write it on your own below.

Instrucciones: Traza cada letra. Luego escríbalo abajo.

Uppercase D

D D D D

A a b c d e f g h i

B j

Name: ____________________ Date: ________________

Directions: Trace each letter. Then write it on your own below.

Instrucciones: Traza cada letra. Luego escríbalo abajo.

Lowercase d

d d d d

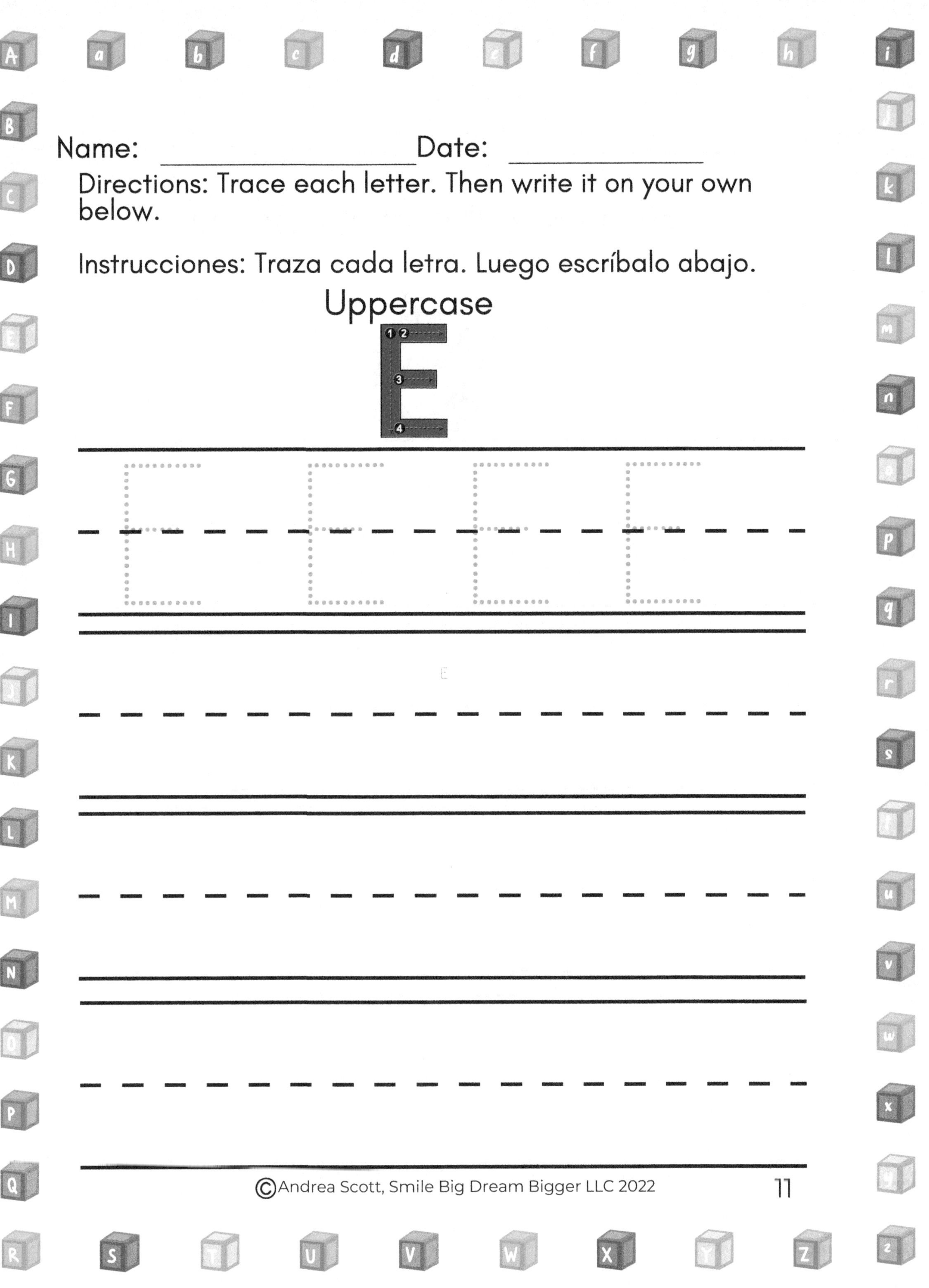

Name: ____________________ Date: ______________

Directions: Trace each letter. Then write it on your own below.

Instrucciones: Traza cada letra. Luego escríbalo abajo.

Uppercase

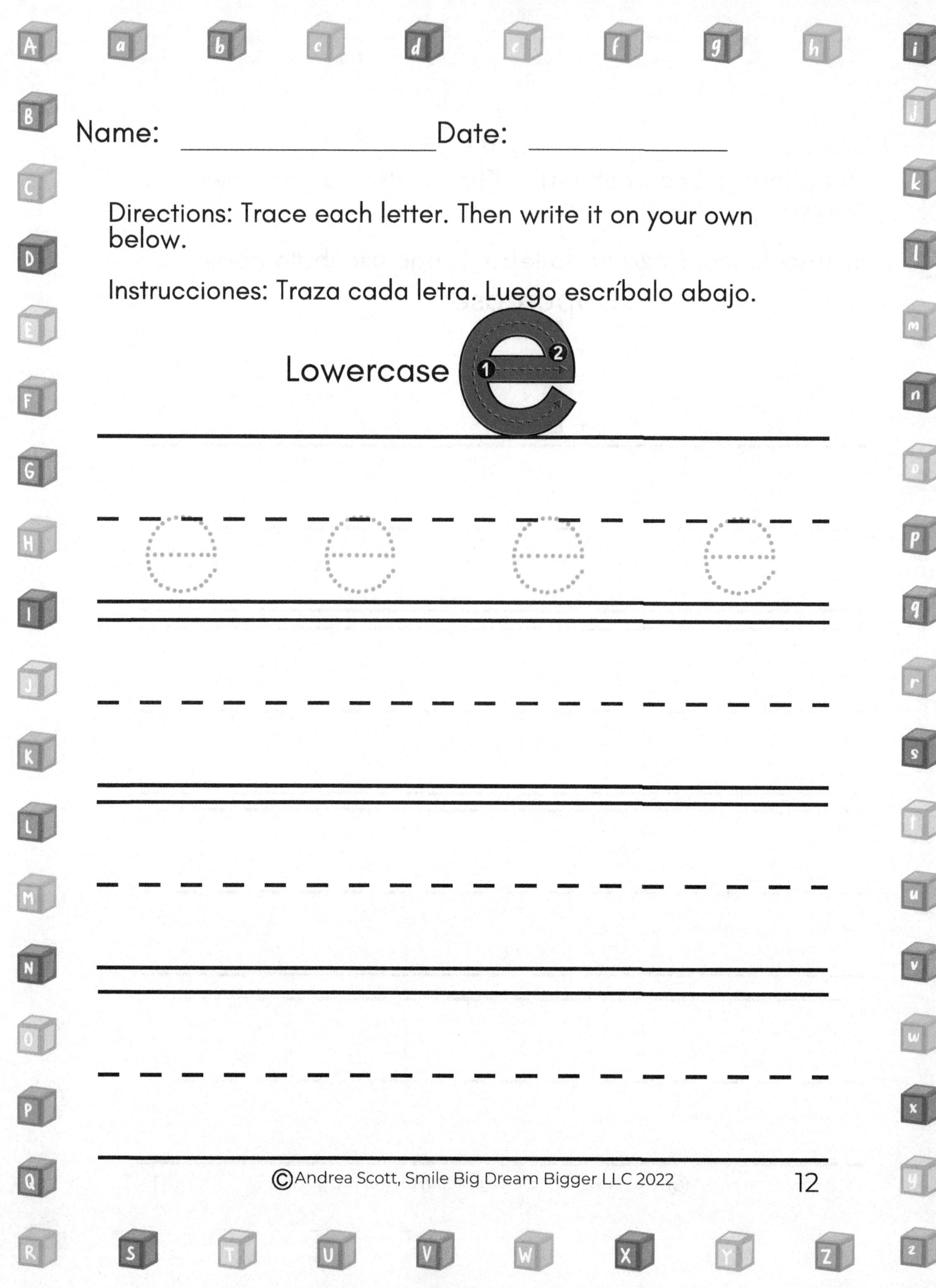

Name: ____________________ Date: ________________

Directions: Trace each letter. Then write it on your own below.

Instructions: Traza cada letra. Luego escríbalo abajo.

Lowercase e

e e e e

Name: ________________ Date: ____________

Directions: Trace each letter. Then write it on your own below.

Instrucciones: Traza cada letra. Luego escríbalo abajo.

Uppercase

F

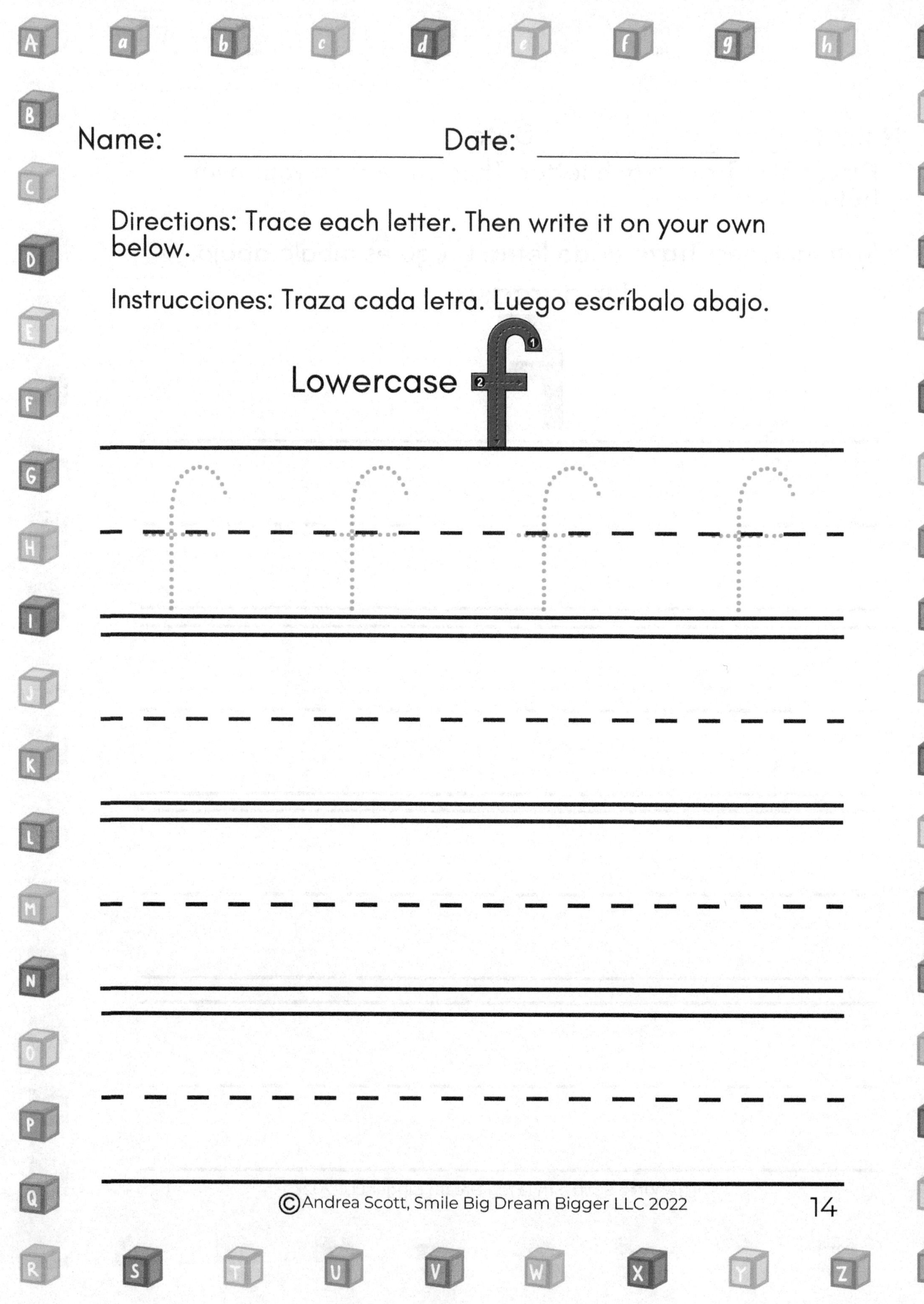

Name: ____________________ Date: ______________

Directions: Trace each letter. Then write it on your own below.

Instrucciones: Traza cada letra. Luego escríbalo abajo.

Lowercase f

f f f f

Name: ________________ Date: ____________

Directions: Trace each letter. Then write it on your own below.

Instrucciones: Traza cada letra. Luego escríbalo abajo.

Uppercase

G

G G G G

Name: ____________________ Date: ______________

Directions: Trace each letter. Then write it on your own below.

Instrucciones: Traza cada letra. Luego escríbalo abajo.

Lowercase g

Name: ____________________ Date: ______________

Directions: Trace each letter. Then write it on your own below.

Instrucciones: Traza cada letra. Luego escríbalo abajo.

Uppercase

H

Name: ____________________ Date: ______________

Directions: Trace each letter. Then write it on your own below.

Instrucciones: Traza cada letra. Luego escríbalo abajo.

Lowercase h

h h h h

Name: ________________ Date: ____________

Directions: Trace each letter. Then write it on your own below.

Instrucciones: Traza cada letra. Luego escríbalo abajo.

Uppercase

I

I I I I

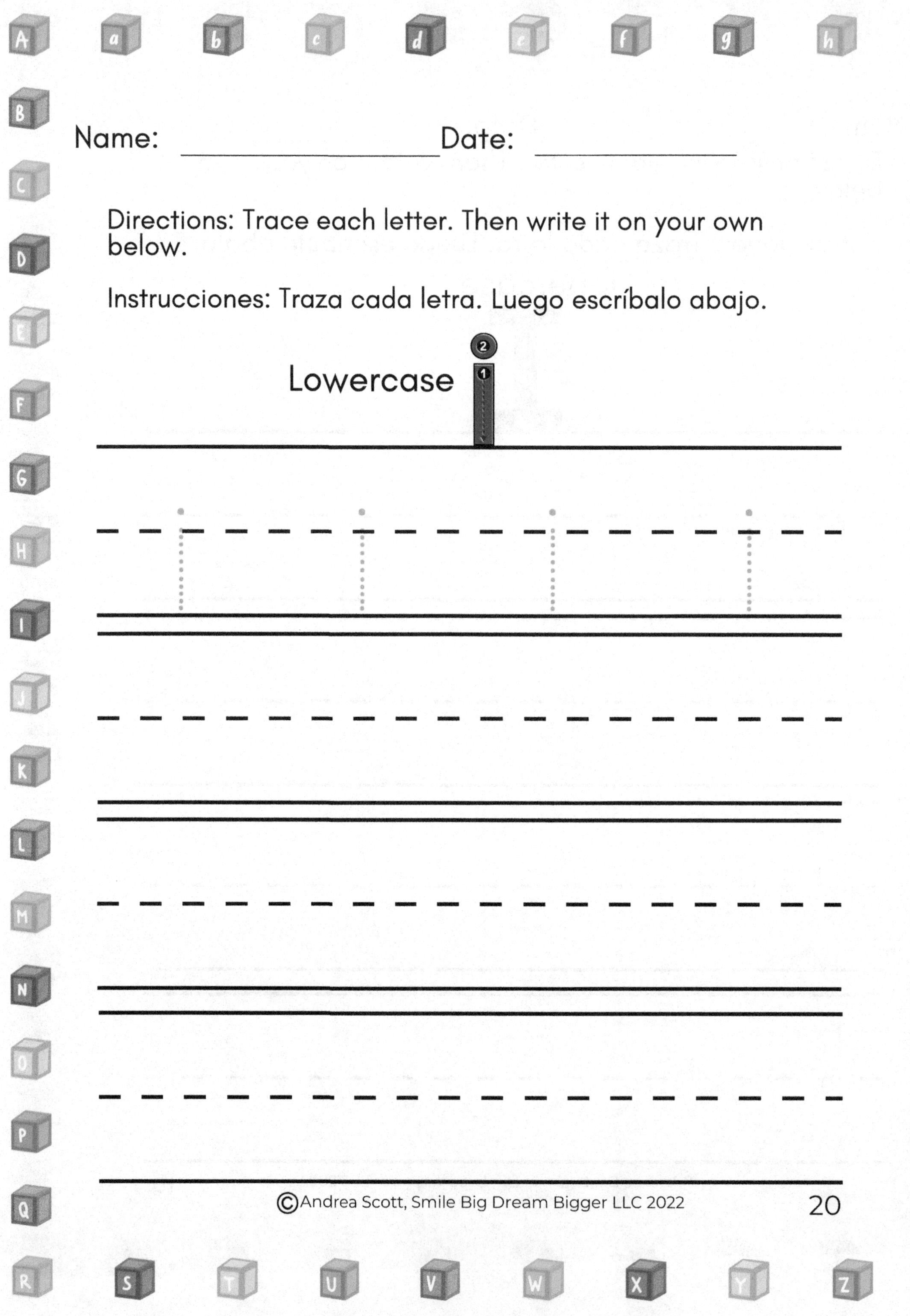

Name: ____________________ Date: ________________

Directions: Trace each letter. Then write it on your own below.

Instrucciones: Traza cada letra. Luego escríbalo abajo.

Lowercase

Name: ________________ Date: ____________

Directions: Trace each letter. Then write it on your own below.

Instrucciones: Traza cada letra. Luego escríbalo abajo.

Uppercase

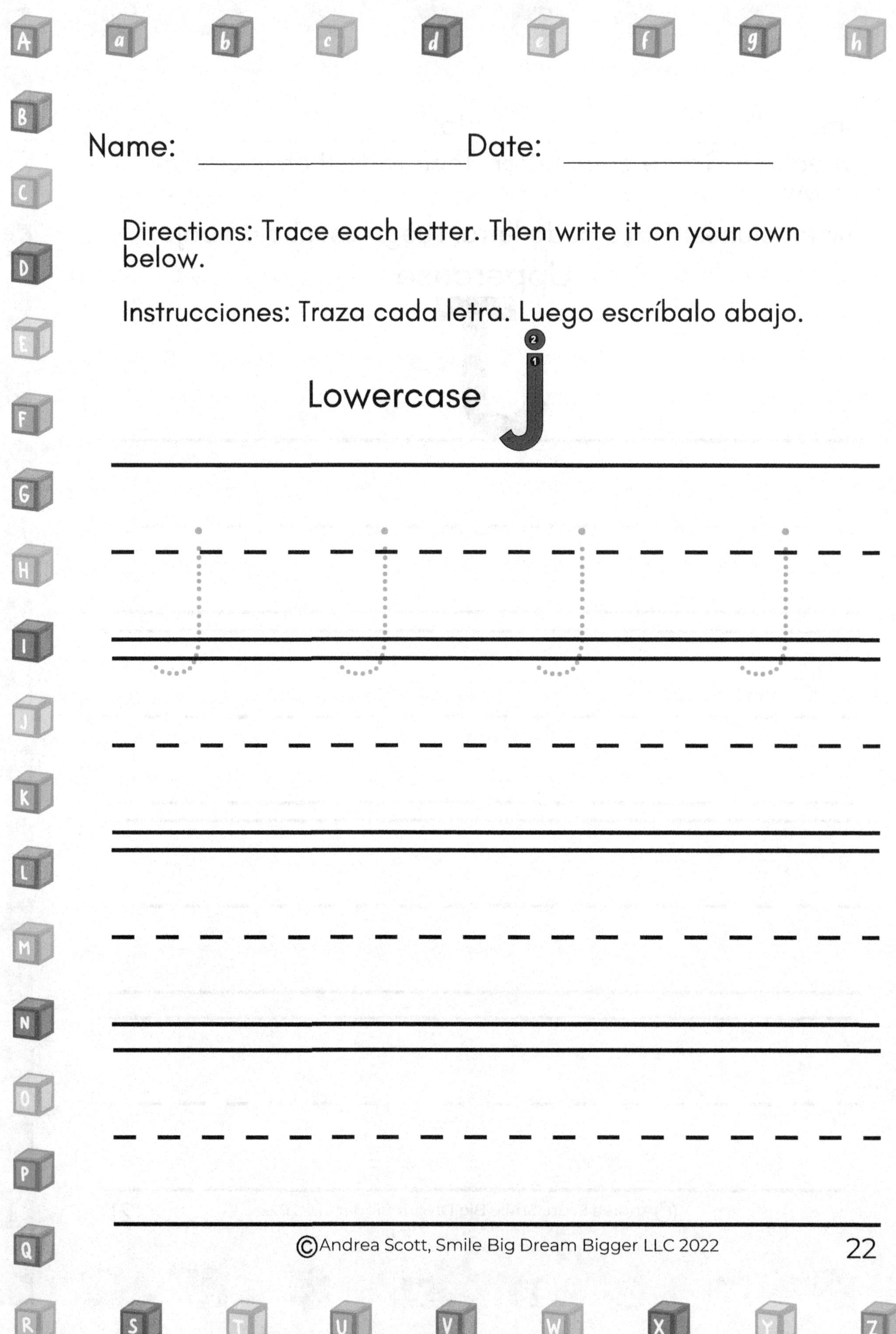

Name: ____________________ Date: ______________

Directions: Trace each letter. Then write it on your own below.

Instrucciones: Traza cada letra. Luego escríbalo abajo.

Lowercase j

Name: ________________ Date: ____________

Directions: Trace each letter. Then write it on your own below.

Instrucciones: Traza cada letra. Luego escríbalo abajo.

Uppercase

K

K K K K

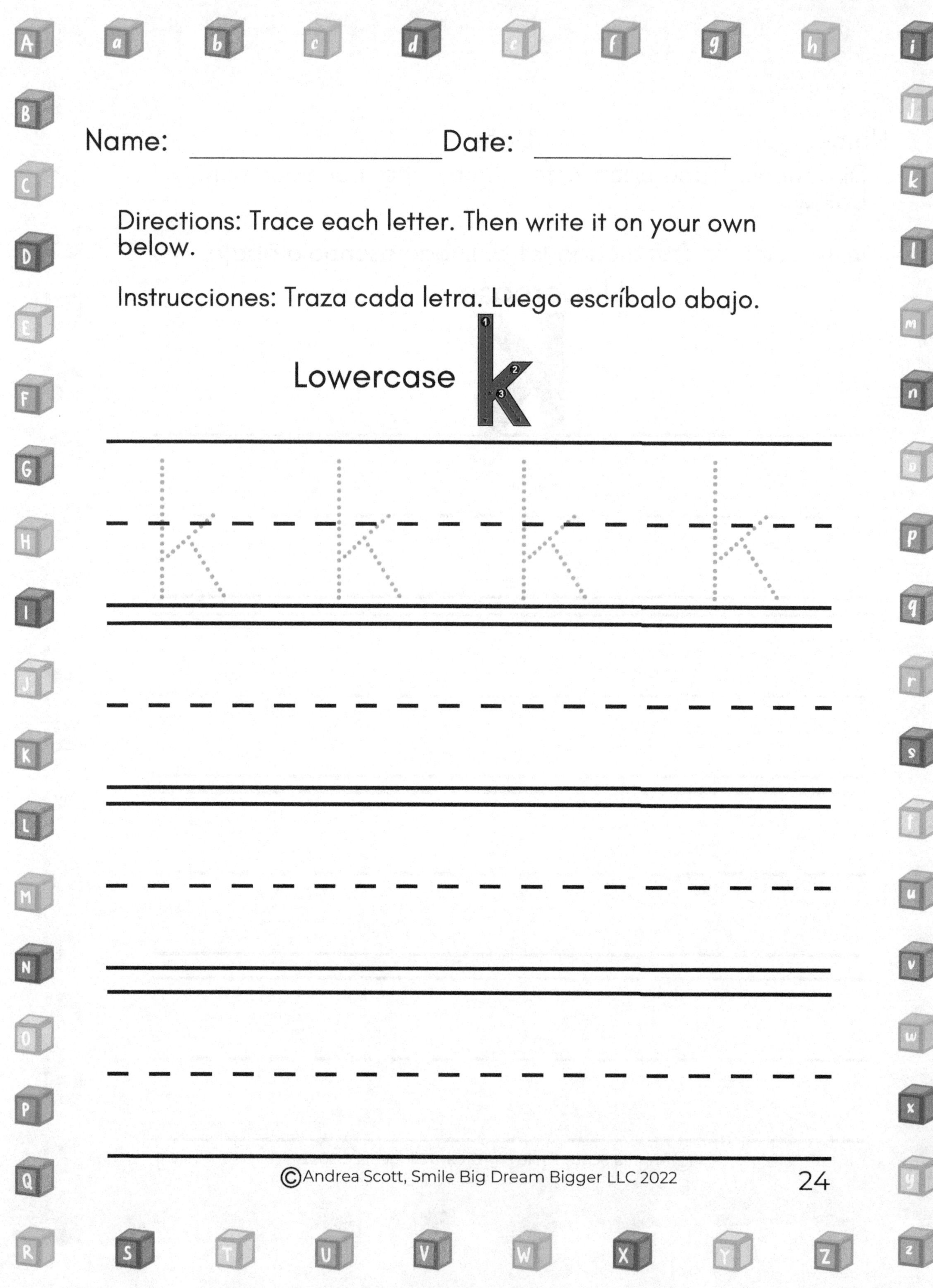

Name: ____________________ Date: ______________

Directions: Trace each letter. Then write it on your own below.

Instrucciones: Traza cada letra. Luego escríbalo abajo.

Lowercase k

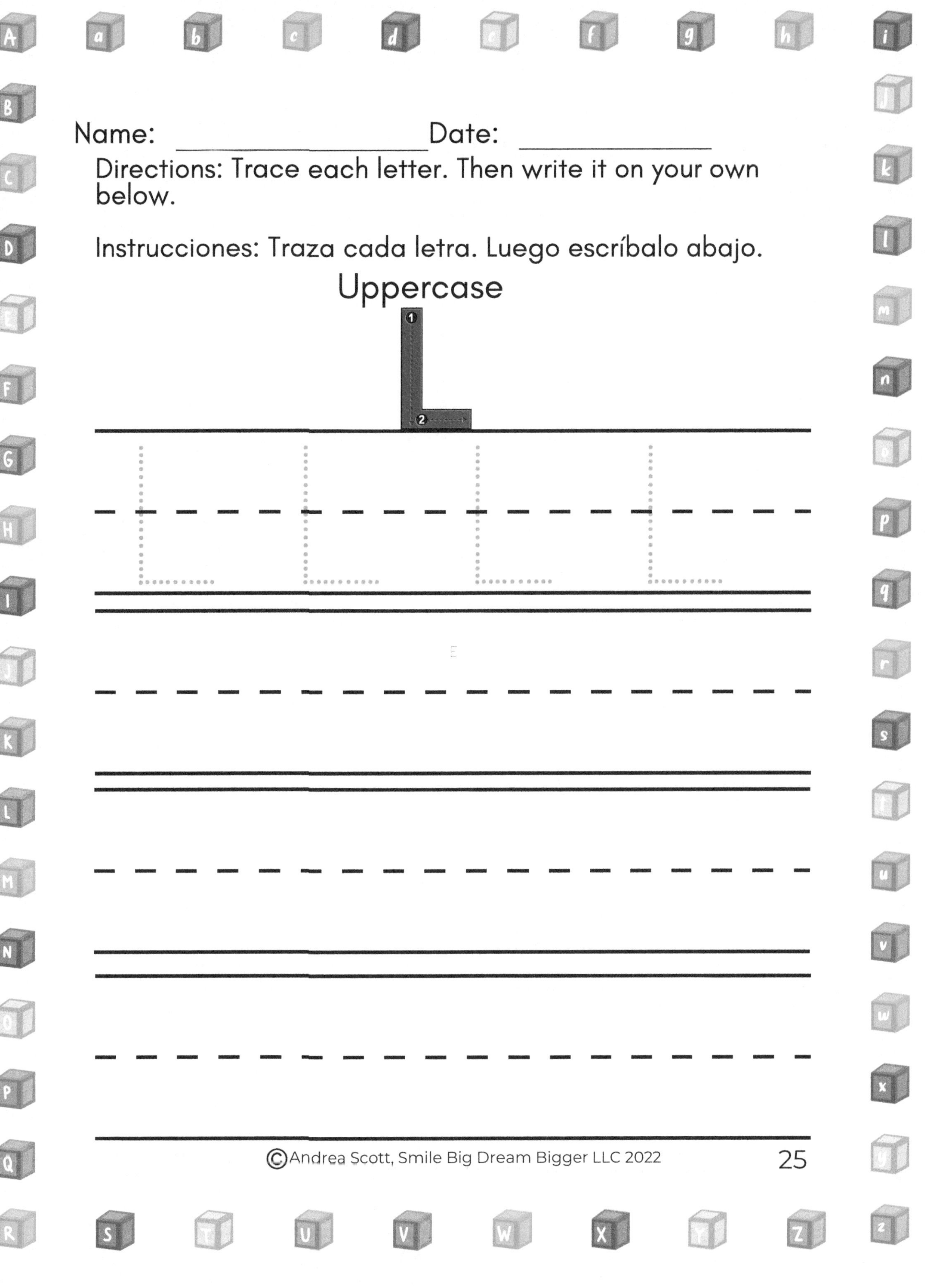

Name: ____________________ Date: ______________

Directions: Trace each letter. Then write it on your own below.

Instrucciones: Traza cada letra. Luego escríbalo abajo.

Uppercase

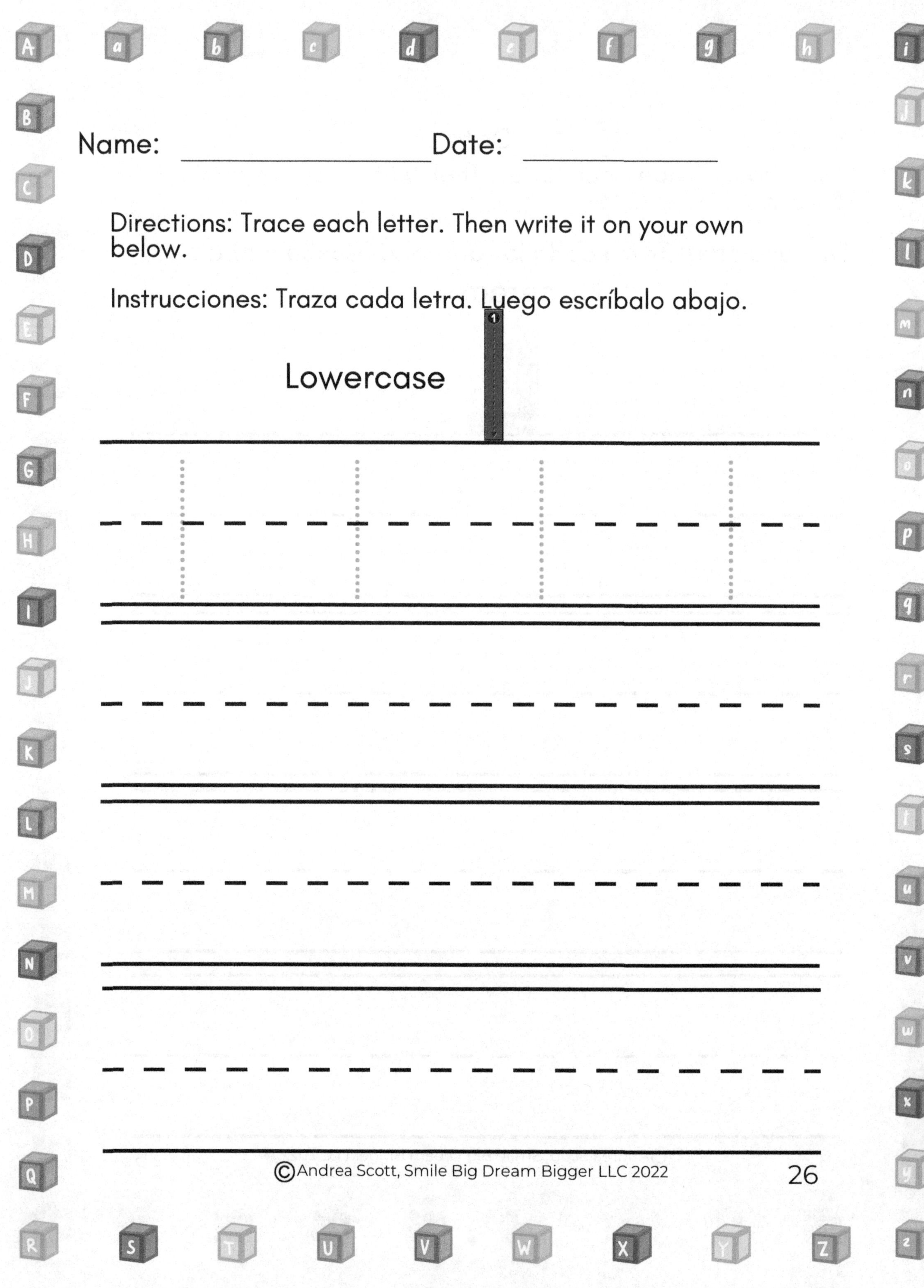

Name: __________________ Date: ______________

Directions: Trace each letter. Then write it on your own below.

Instrucciones: Traza cada letra. Luego escríbalo abajo.

Lowercase

Name: ________________ Date: ____________

Directions: Trace each letter. Then write it on your own below.

Instrucciones: Traza cada letra. Luego escríbalo abajo.

Uppercase

M

M M M M

Name: ____________________ Date: ______________

Directions: Trace each letter. Then write it on your own below.

Instructions: Traza cada letra. Luego escríbalo abajo.

Lowercase m

m m m m

Name: ______________ Date: ____________

Directions: Trace each letter. Then write it on your own below.

Instrucciones: Traza cada letra. Luego escríbalo abajo.

Uppercase

N N N N

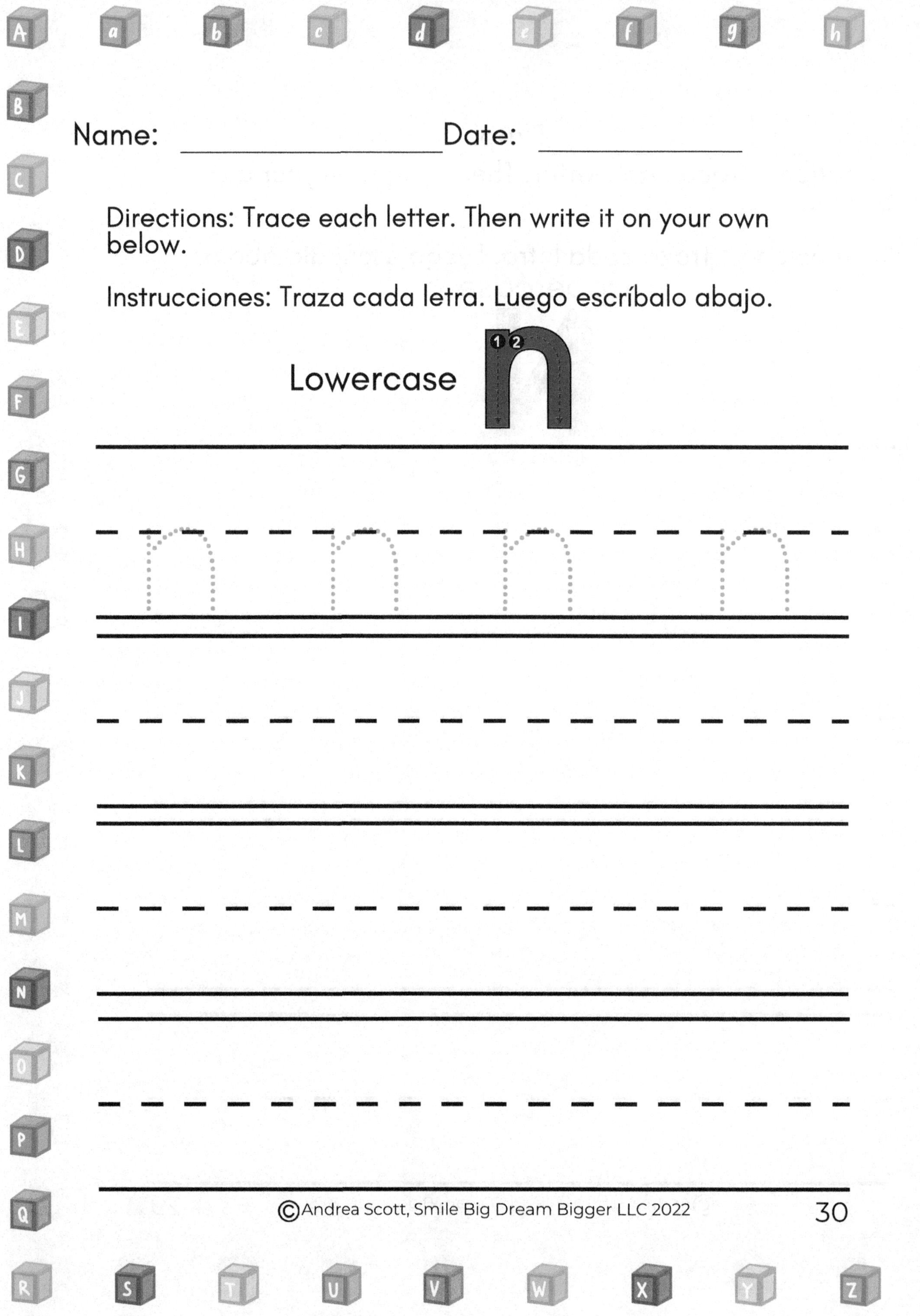

Name: ____________________ Date: ______________

Directions: Trace each letter. Then write it on your own below.

Instrucciones: Traza cada letra. Luego escríbalo abajo.

Lowercase n

n n n n

Name: ___________________ Date: _______________

Directions: Trace each letter. Then write it on your own below.

Instrucciones: Traza cada letra. Luego escríbalo abajo.

Uppercase

O

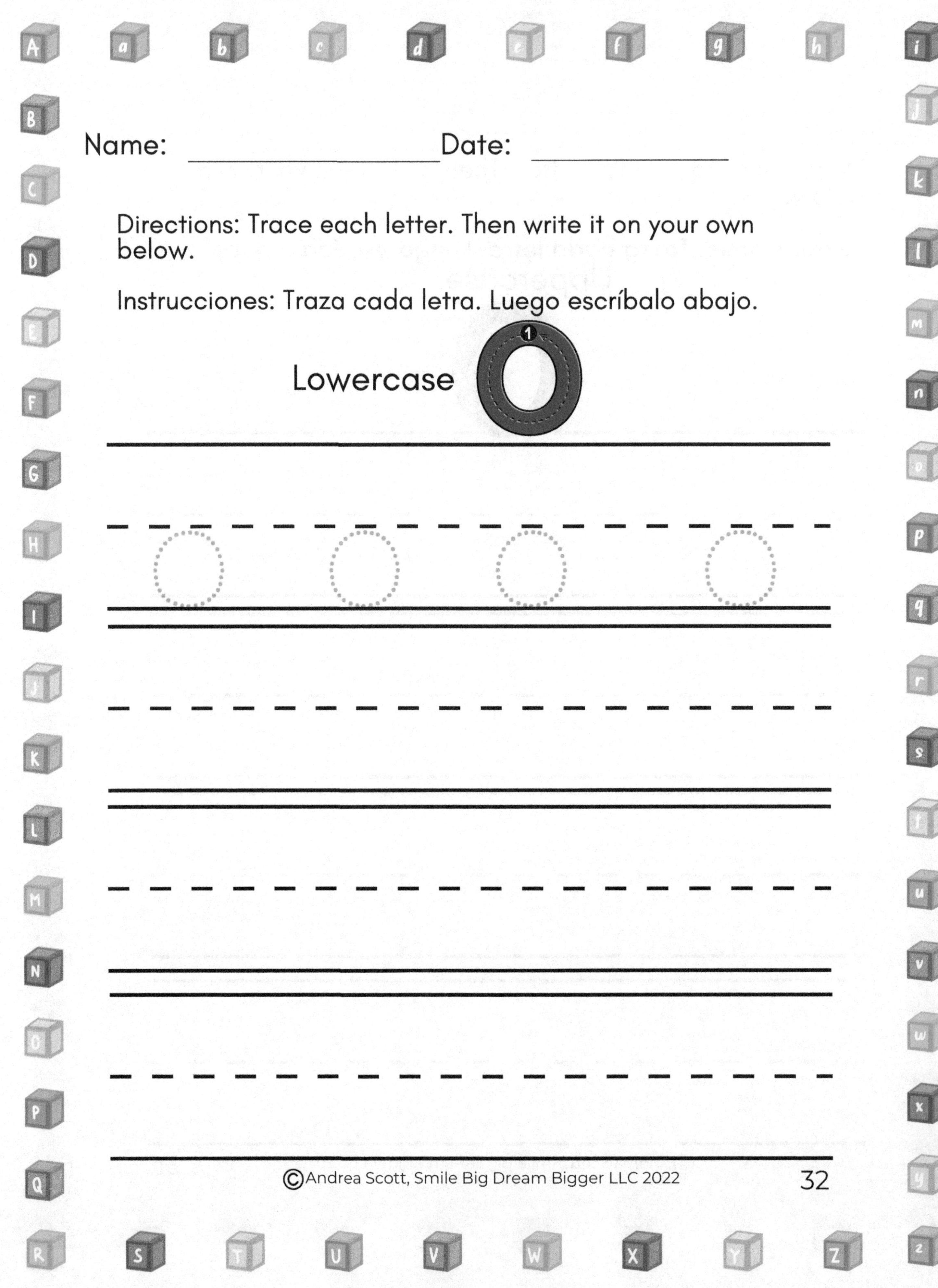

Name: ____________________ Date: ______________

Directions: Trace each letter. Then write it on your own below.

Instrucciones: Traza cada letra. Luego escríbalo abajo.

Lowercase o

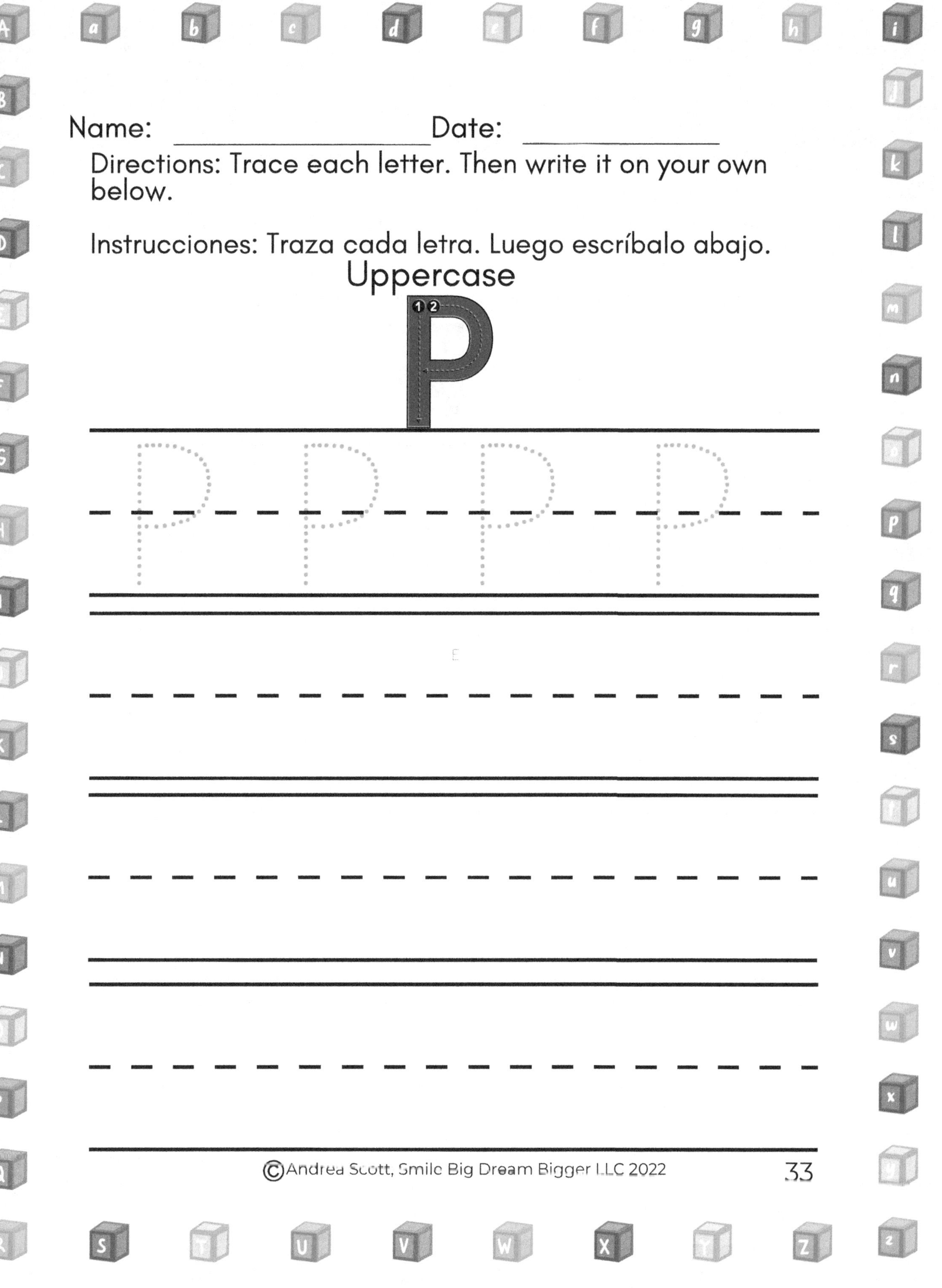

Name: ________________ Date: ____________

Directions: Trace each letter. Then write it on your own below.

Instrucciones: Traza cada letra. Luego escríbalo abajo.

Uppercase

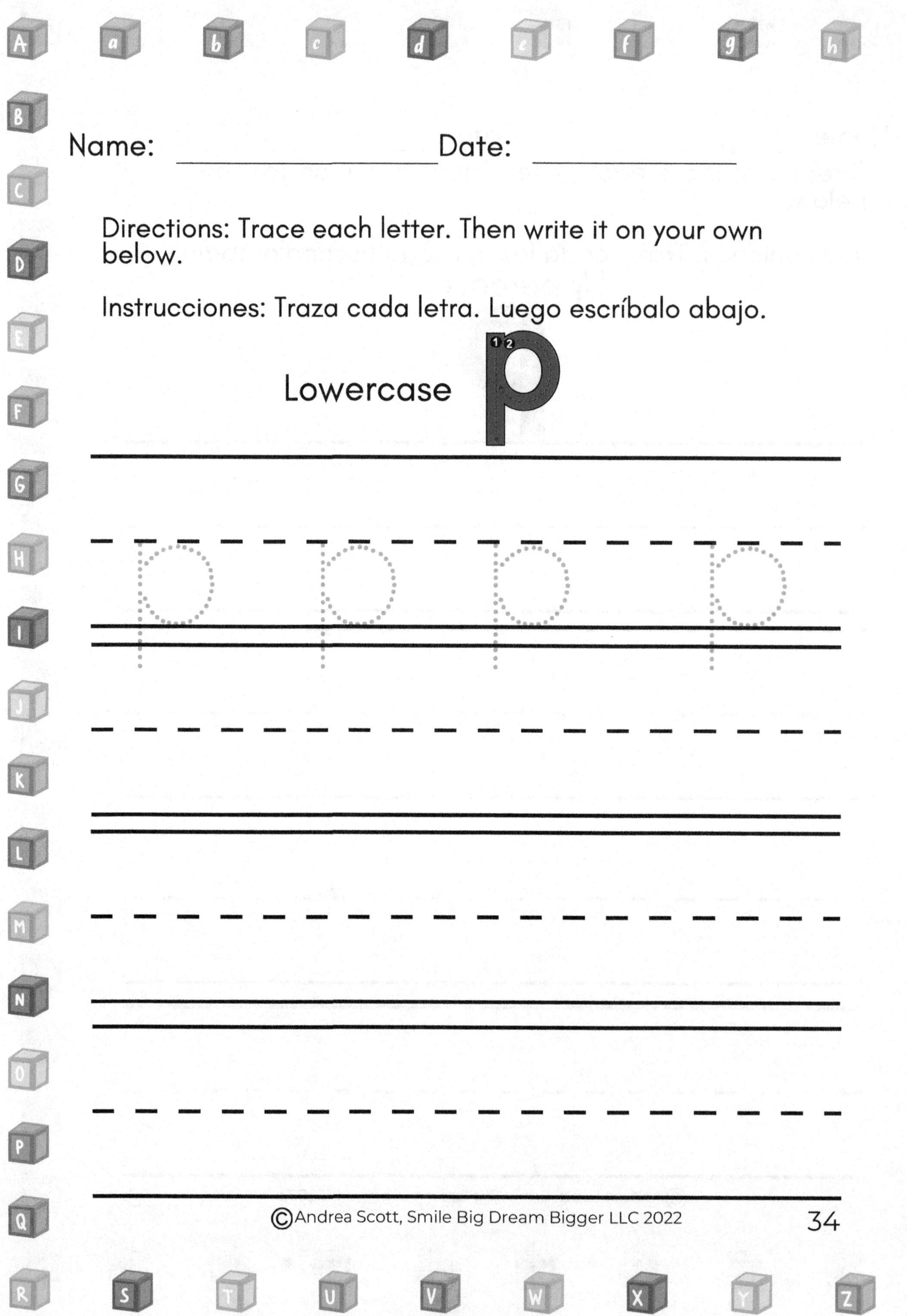

Name: ____________________ Date: ______________

Directions: Trace each letter. Then write it on your own below.

Instrucciones: Traza cada letra. Luego escríbalo abajo.

Lowercase p

Name: ________________ Date: ____________

Directions: Trace each letter. Then write it on your own below.

Instrucciones: Traza cada letra. Luego escríbalo abajo.

Uppercase

Q

Q Q Q Q

Name: ____________________ Date: ______________

Directions: Trace each letter. Then write it on your own below.

Instructions: Traza cada letra. Luego escríbalo abajo.

Lowercase q

Name: ____________________ Date: ______________

Directions: Trace each letter. Then write it on your own below.

Instrucciones: Traza cada letra. Luego escríbalo abajo.

Uppercase

R

R R R R

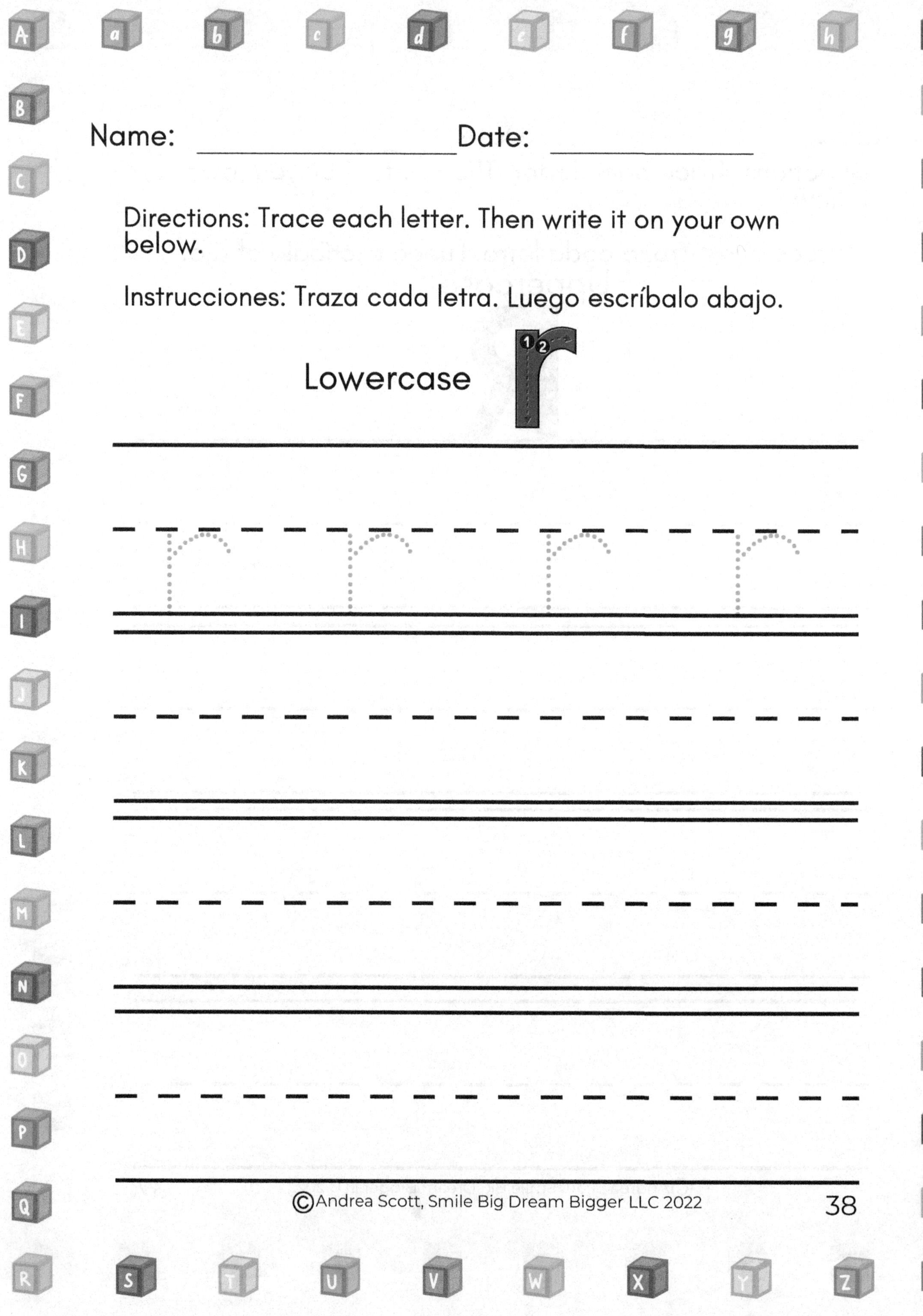

Name: ____________________ Date: ______________

Directions: Trace each letter. Then write it on your own below.

Instrucciones: Traza cada letra. Luego escríbalo abajo.

Lowercase r

r r r r

Name: ________________ Date: ____________

Directions: Trace each letter. Then write it on your own below.

Instrucciones: Traza cada letra. Luego escríbalo abajo.

Uppercase

S

S S S S

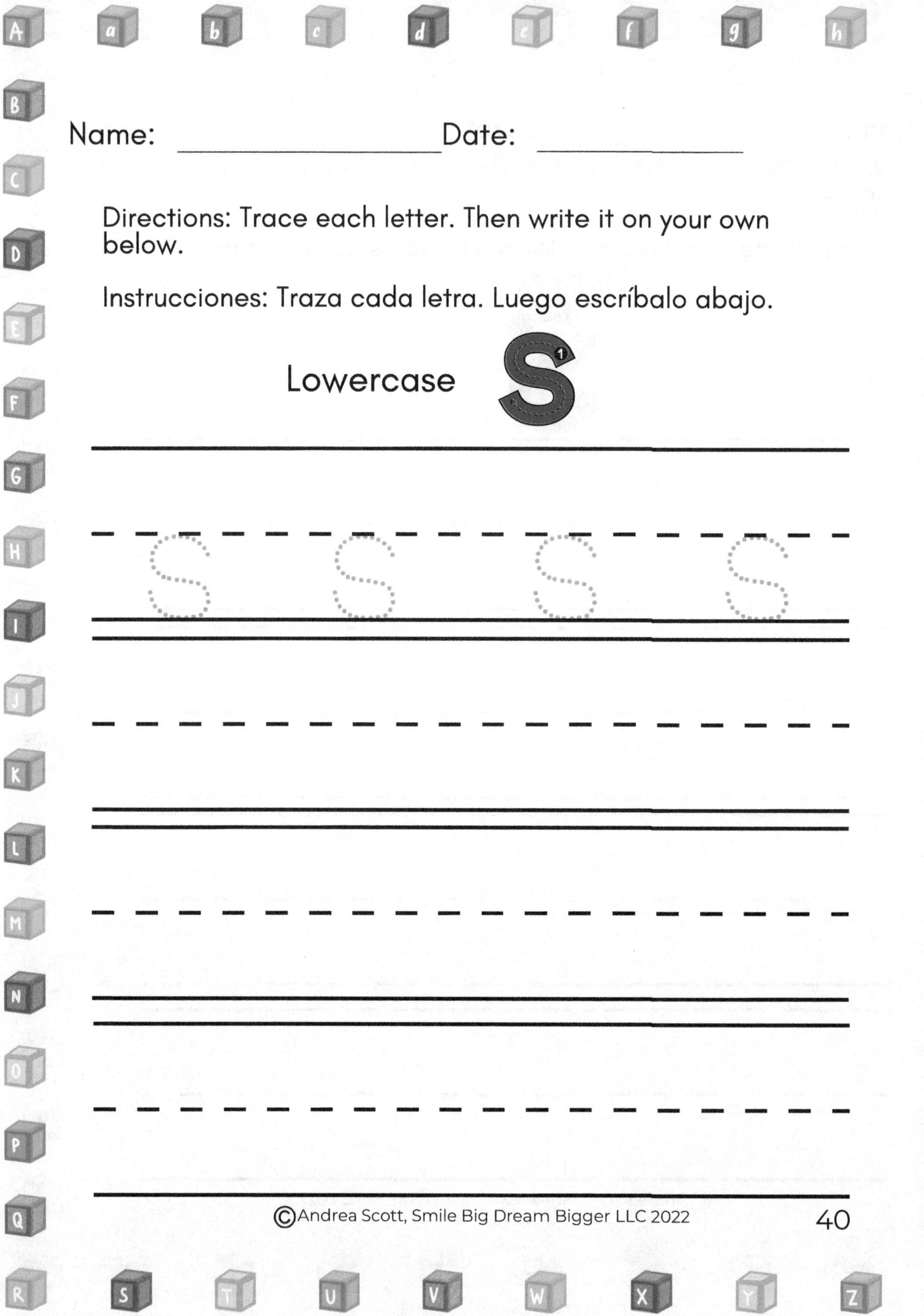

Name: ____________________ Date: ______________

Directions: Trace each letter. Then write it on your own below.

Instrucciones: Traza cada letra. Luego escríbalo abajo.

Lowercase s

s s s s

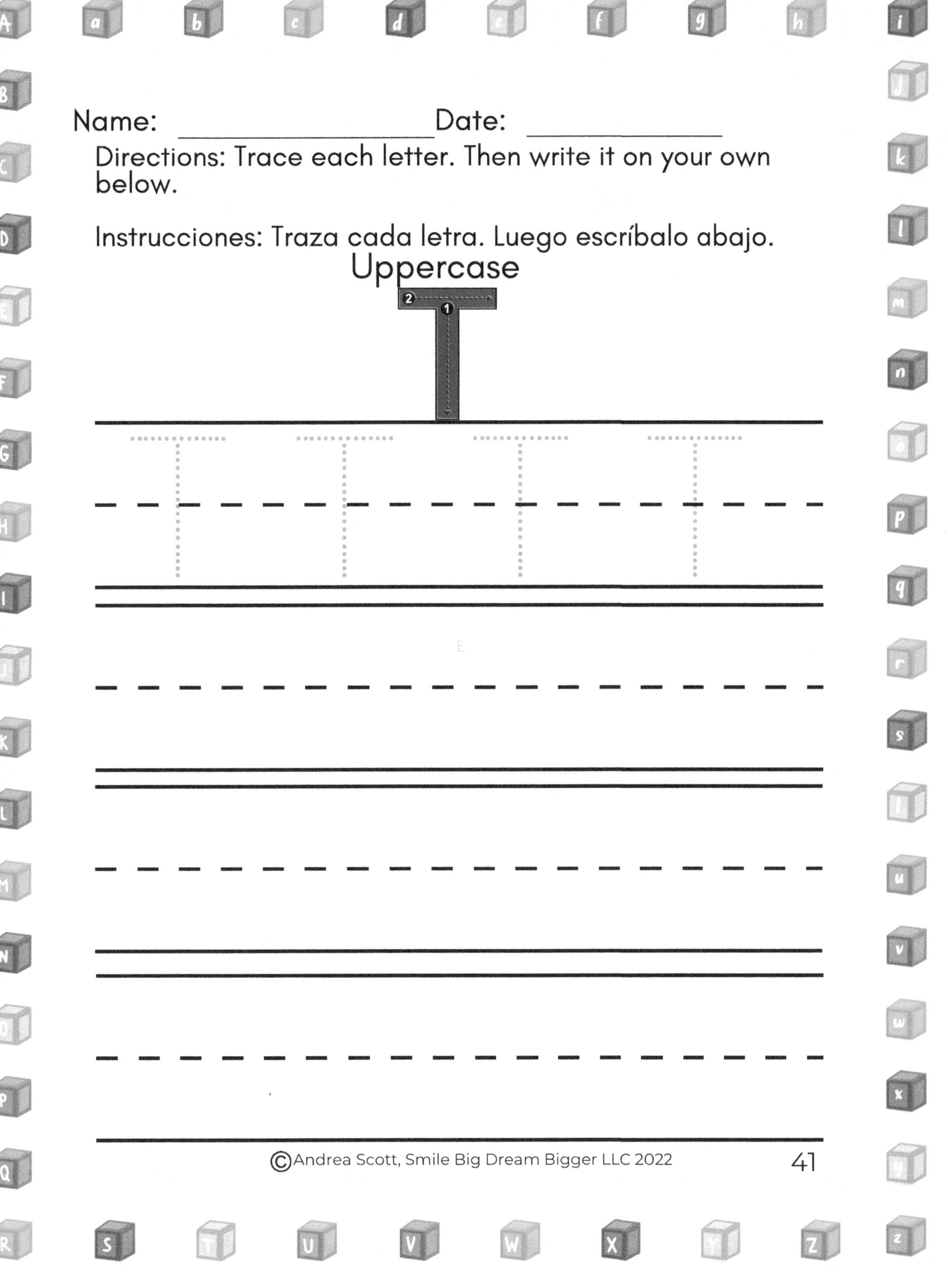

Name: ____________________ Date: ______________

Directions: Trace each letter. Then write it on your own below.

Instrucciones: Traza cada letra. Luego escríbalo abajo.

Uppercase

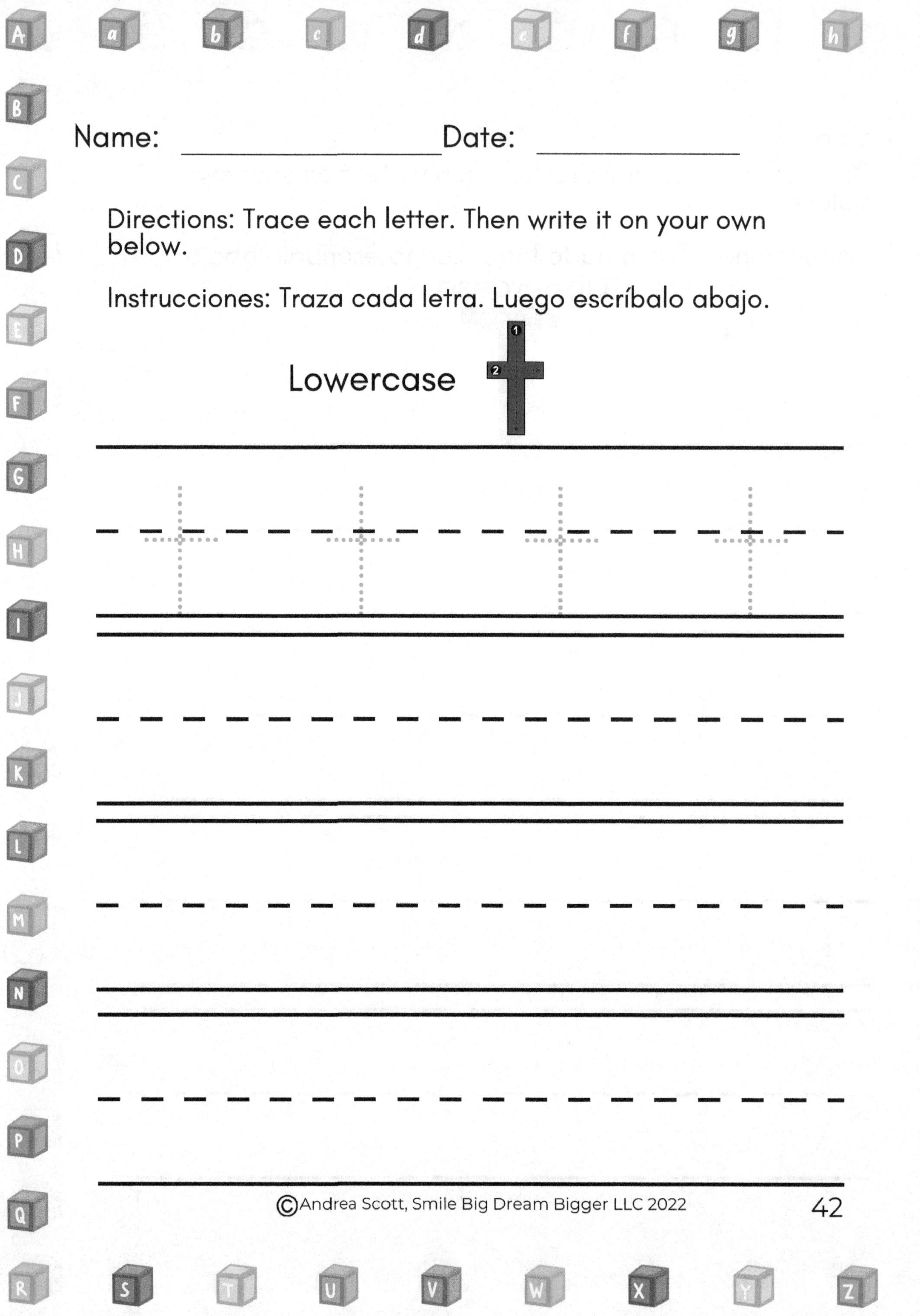

Name: ____________________ Date: ________________

Directions: Trace each letter. Then write it on your own below.

Instrucciones: Traza cada letra. Luego escríbalo abajo.

Lowercase

Name: ________________ Date: ____________

Directions: Trace each letter. Then write it on your own below.

Instrucciones: Traza cada letra. Luego escríbalo abajo.

Uppercase

U

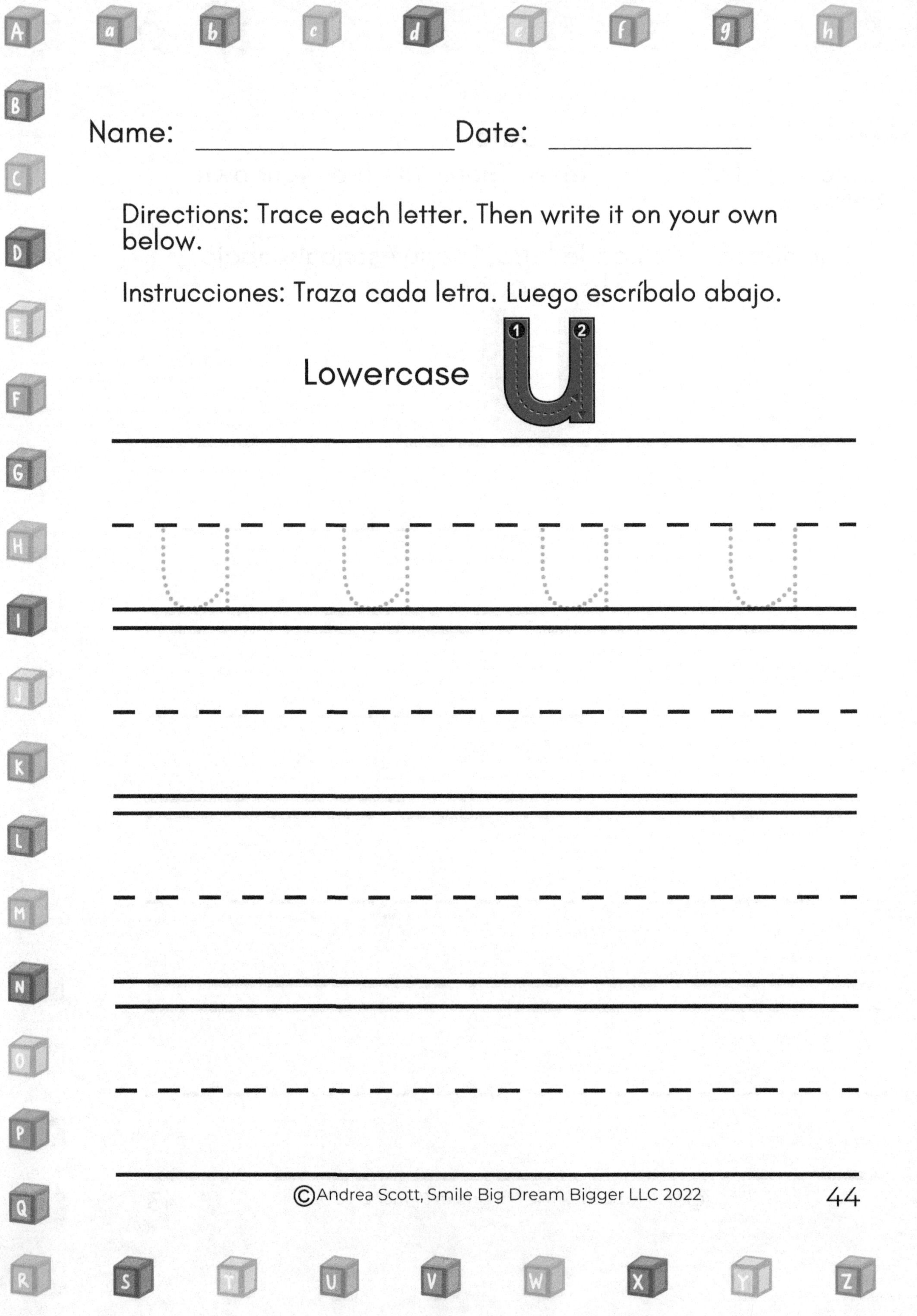

Name: ____________________ Date: ________________

Directions: Trace each letter. Then write it on your own below.

Instrucciones: Traza cada letra. Luego escríbalo abajo.

Lowercase u

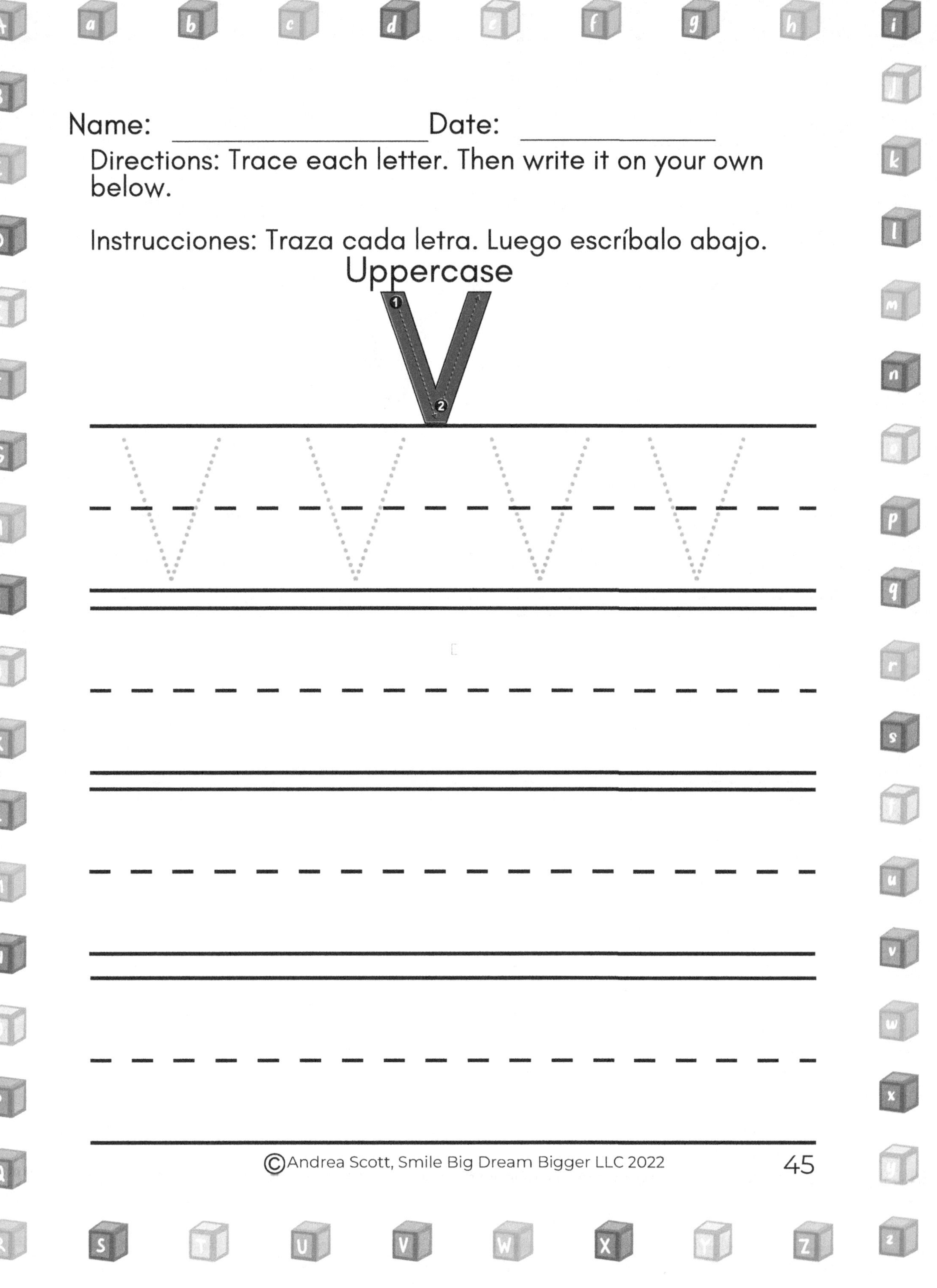

Name: ________________ Date: ____________

Directions: Trace each letter. Then write it on your own below.

Instrucciones: Traza cada letra. Luego escríbalo abajo.

Uppercase

V

A a b c d e f g h i
B j
C k
D l
E m
F n
G o
H p
I q
J r
K s
L t
M u
N v
O w
P x
Q y
R S T U V W X Y Z z

Name: ________________ Date: ____________

Directions: Trace each letter. Then write it on your own below.

Instrucciones: Traza cada letra. Luego escríbalo abajo.

Lowercase v

v v v v

Name: ________________ Date: ____________

Directions: Trace each letter. Then write it on your own below.

Instrucciones: Traza cada letra. Luego escríbalo abajo.

Uppercase

W

W W W W

Name: ________________ Date: ____________

Directions: Trace each letter. Then write it on your own below.

Instrucciones: Traza cada letra. Luego escríbalo abajo.

Lowercase w

w w w w

Name: _______________ Date: ___________

Directions: Trace each letter. Then write it on your own below.

Instrucciones: Traza cada letra. Luego escríbalo abajo.

Uppercase

X

X X X X

Name: ____________________ Date: ______________

Directions: Trace each letter. Then write it on your own below.

Instrucciones: Traza cada letra. Luego escríbalo abajo.

Lowercase x

x x x x

Name: ____________________ Date: ______________

Directions: Trace each letter. Then write it on your own below.

Instrucciones: Traza cada letra. Luego escríbalo abajo.

Uppercase

Y

Name: ____________________ Date: ______________

Directions: Trace each letter. Then write it on your own below.

Instructions: Traza cada letra. Luego escríbalo abajo.

Lowercase y

y y y y

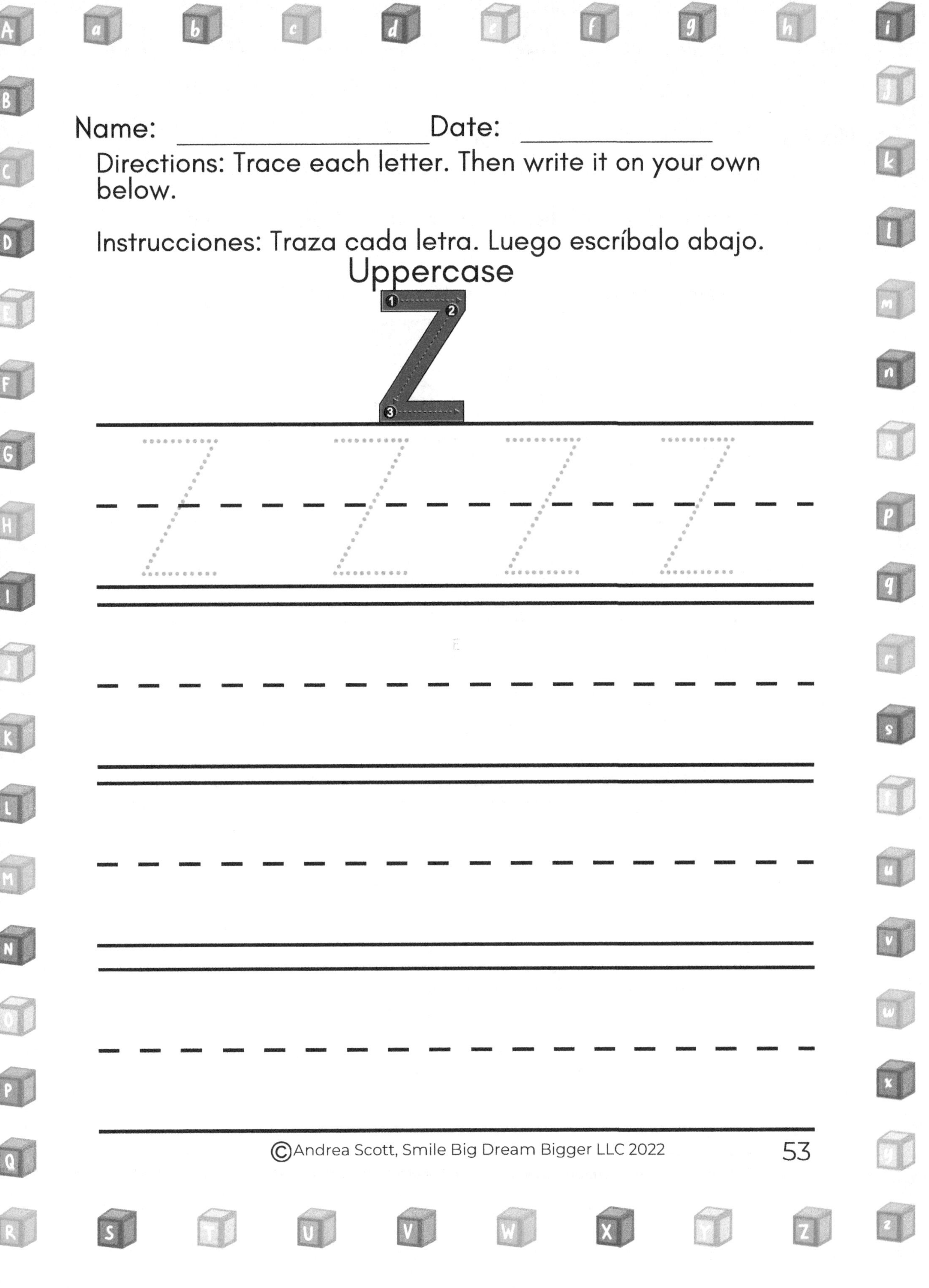

Name: ____________________ Date: ______________

Directions: Trace each letter. Then write it on your own below.

Instrucciones: Traza cada letra. Luego escríbalo abajo.

Uppercase

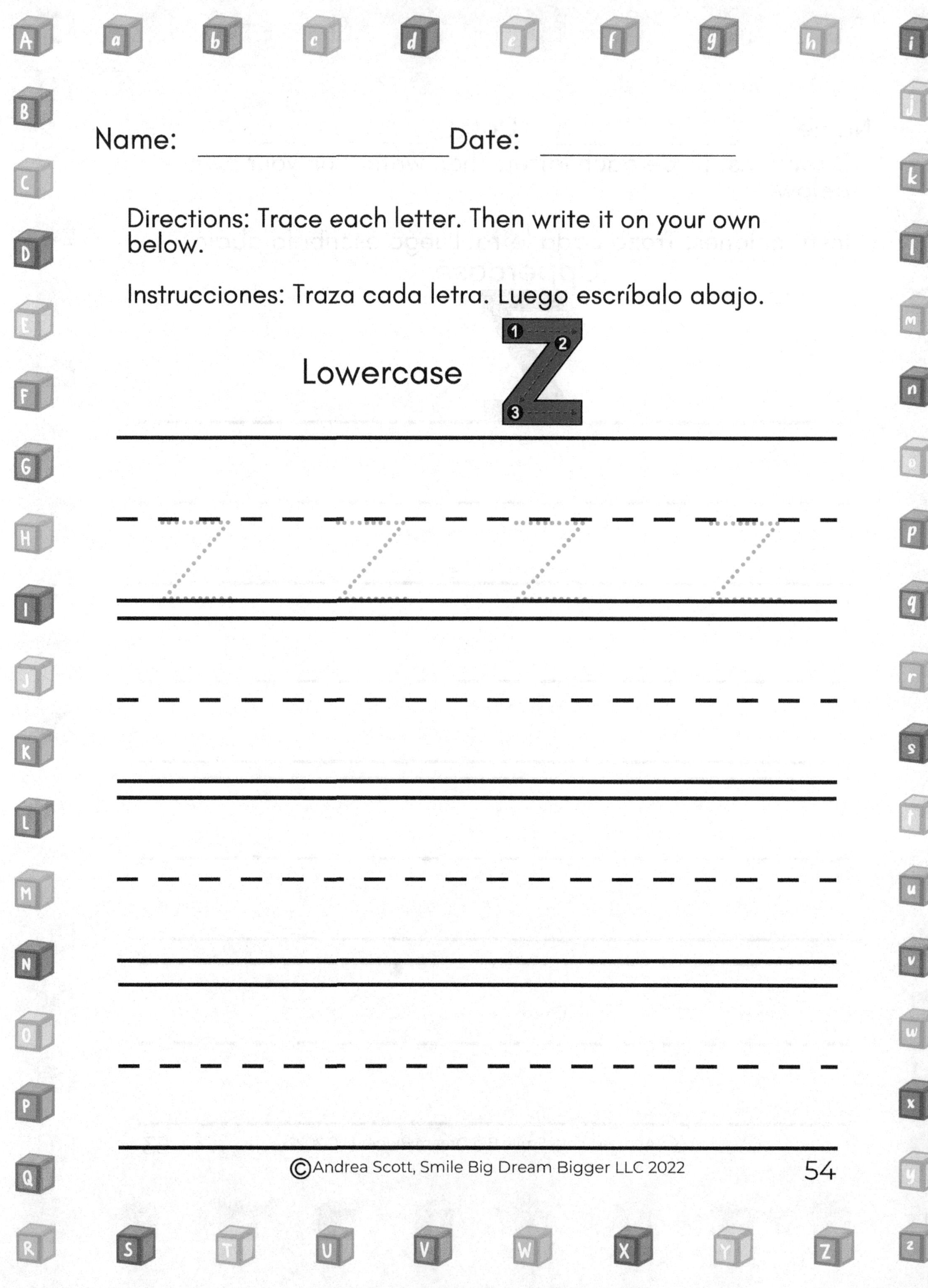

Name: ____________________ Date: ______________

Directions: Trace each letter. Then write it on your own below.

Instrucciones: Traza cada letra. Luego escríbalo abajo.

Lowercase z

Name: ____________________ Date: ______________

Directions: Circle the pictures that start with the letter A.

Instrucciones: Encierra las imágenes que comienzan con la letra A.

Aa

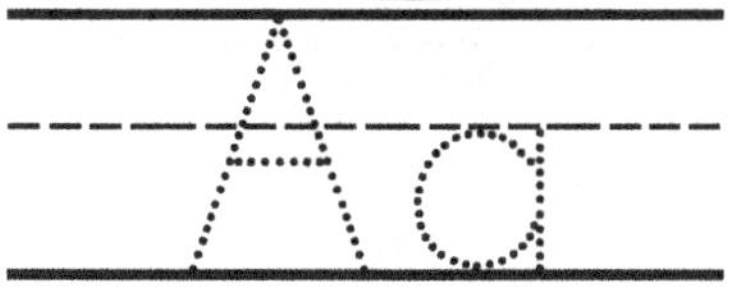

Aa

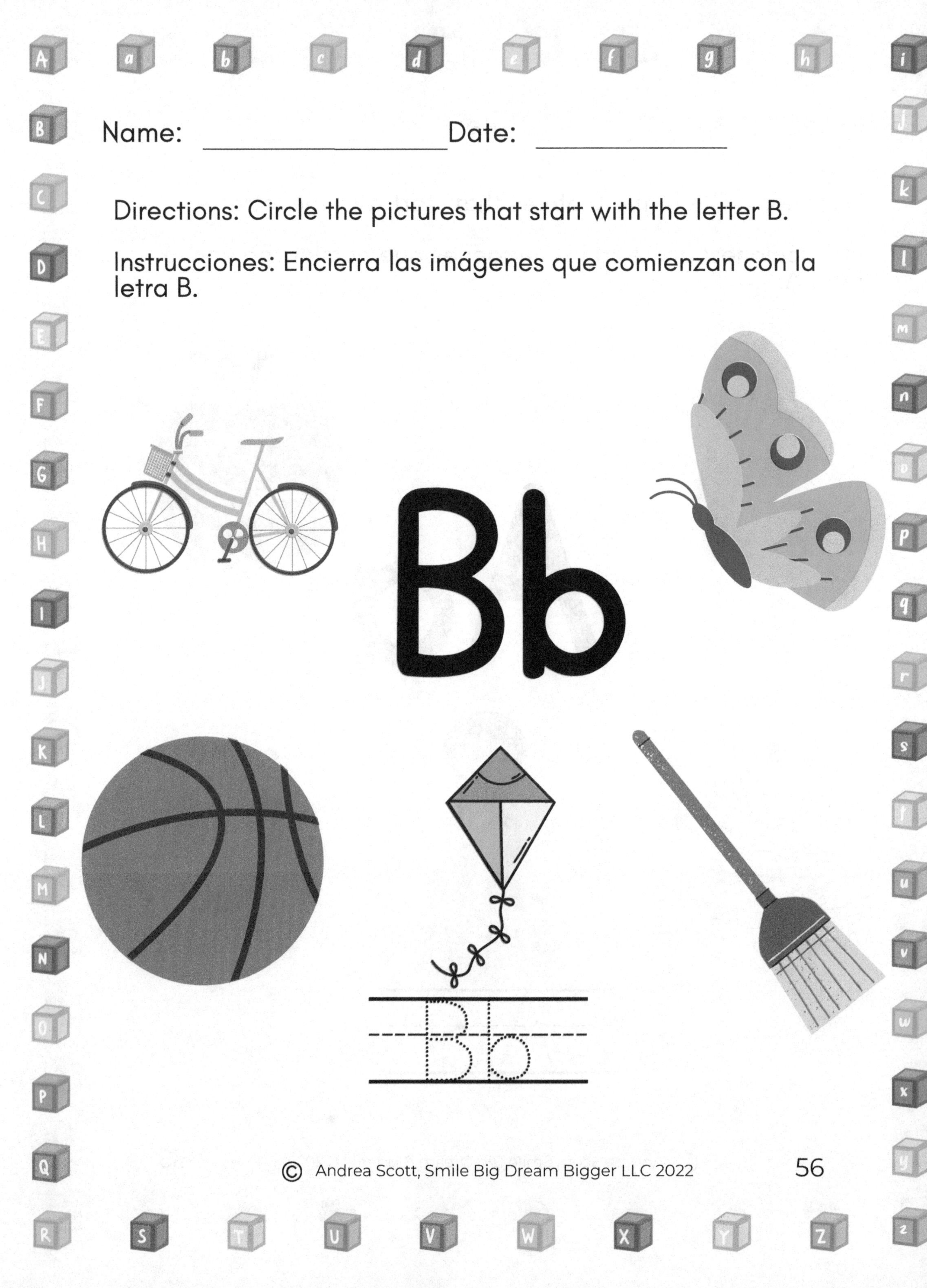

Name: ____________________ Date: ______________

Directions: Circle the pictures that start with the letter B.

Instrucciones: Encierra las imágenes que comienzan con la letra B.

Name: ______________________ Date: ________________

Directions: Circle the pictures that start with the letter C.

Instrucciones: Encierra las imágenes que comienzan con la letra C.

Cc

Name: ____________________ Date: ______________

Directions: Circle the pictures that start with the letter D.

Instrucciones: Encierra las imágenes que comienzan con la letra D.

Dd

Dd

Name: ___________________ Date: ______________

Directions: Circle the pictures that start with the letter E.

Instrucciones: Encierra las imágenes que comienzan con la letra E.

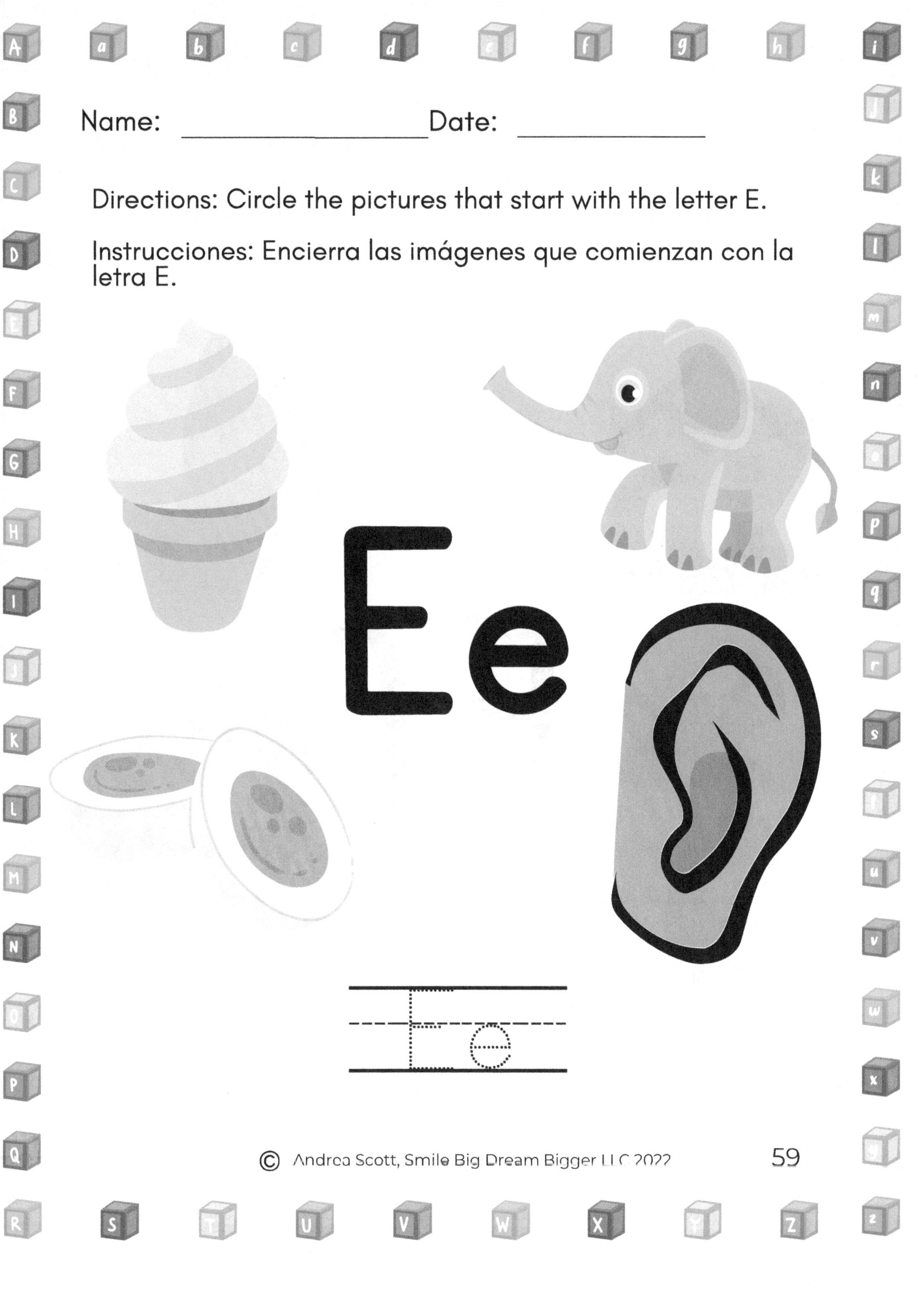

Name: ______________________ Date: _______________

Directions: Circle the pictures that start with the letter F.

Instrucciones: Encierra las imágenes que comienzan con la letra F.

Name: ____________ Date: ____________
Directions: Circle the pictures that start with the letter G.
Instrucciones: Encierra las imágenes que comienzan con la letra G.
ORIGINAL
BUBBLE GUM
Gg
Gg
© Andrea Scott, Smile Big Dream Bigger LLC 2022
61

Name: ____________________ Date: ______________

Directions: Circle the pictures that start with the letter H.

Instrucciones: Encierra las imágenes que comienzan con la letra H.

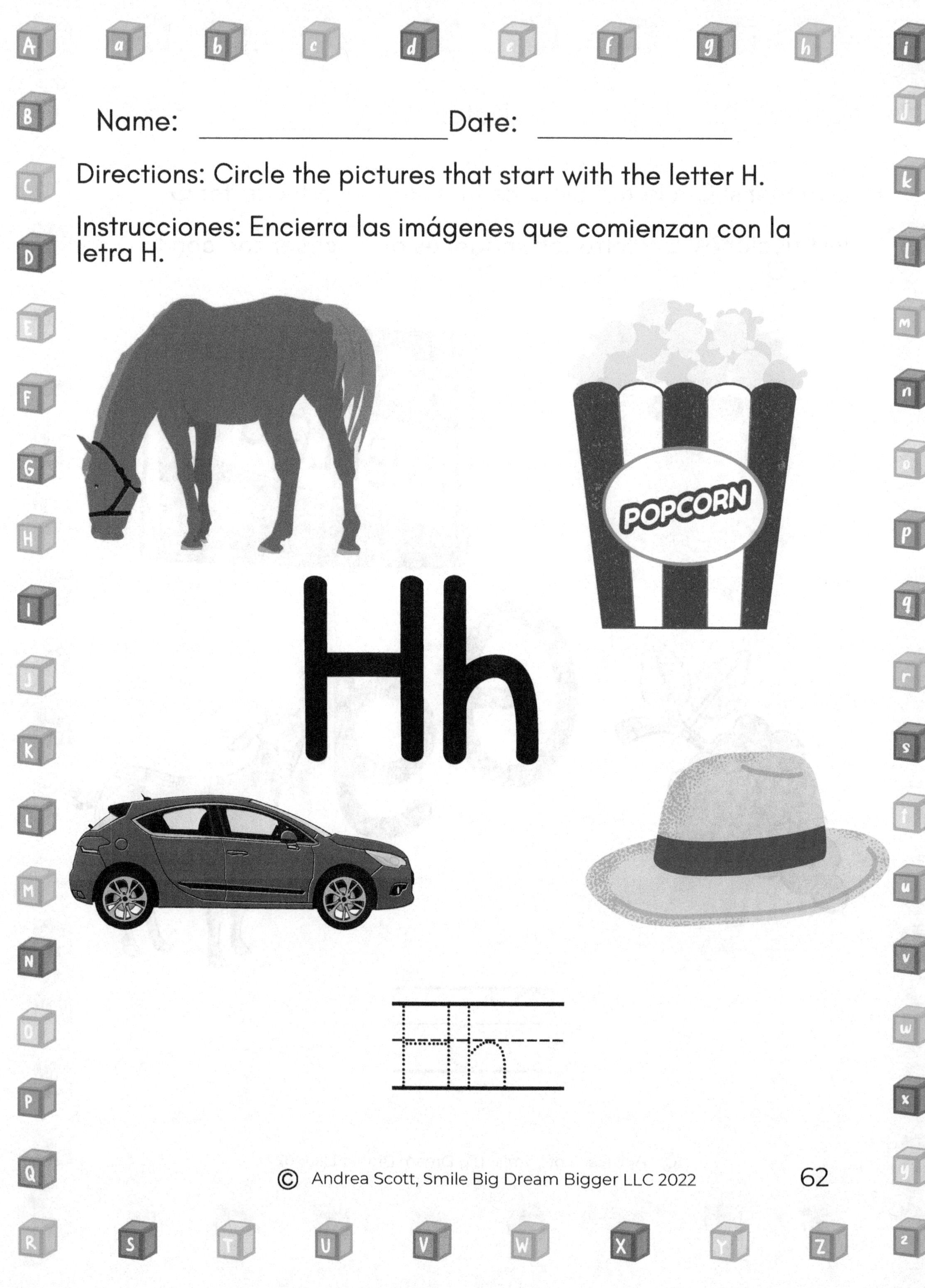

Name: ___________________ Date: _____________

Directions: Circle the pictures that start with the letter I.

Instrucciones: Encierra las imágenes que comienzan con la letra I.

Name: ____________________ Date: ______________

Directions: Circle the pictures that start with the letter J.

Instrucciones: Encierra las imágenes que comienzan con la letra J.

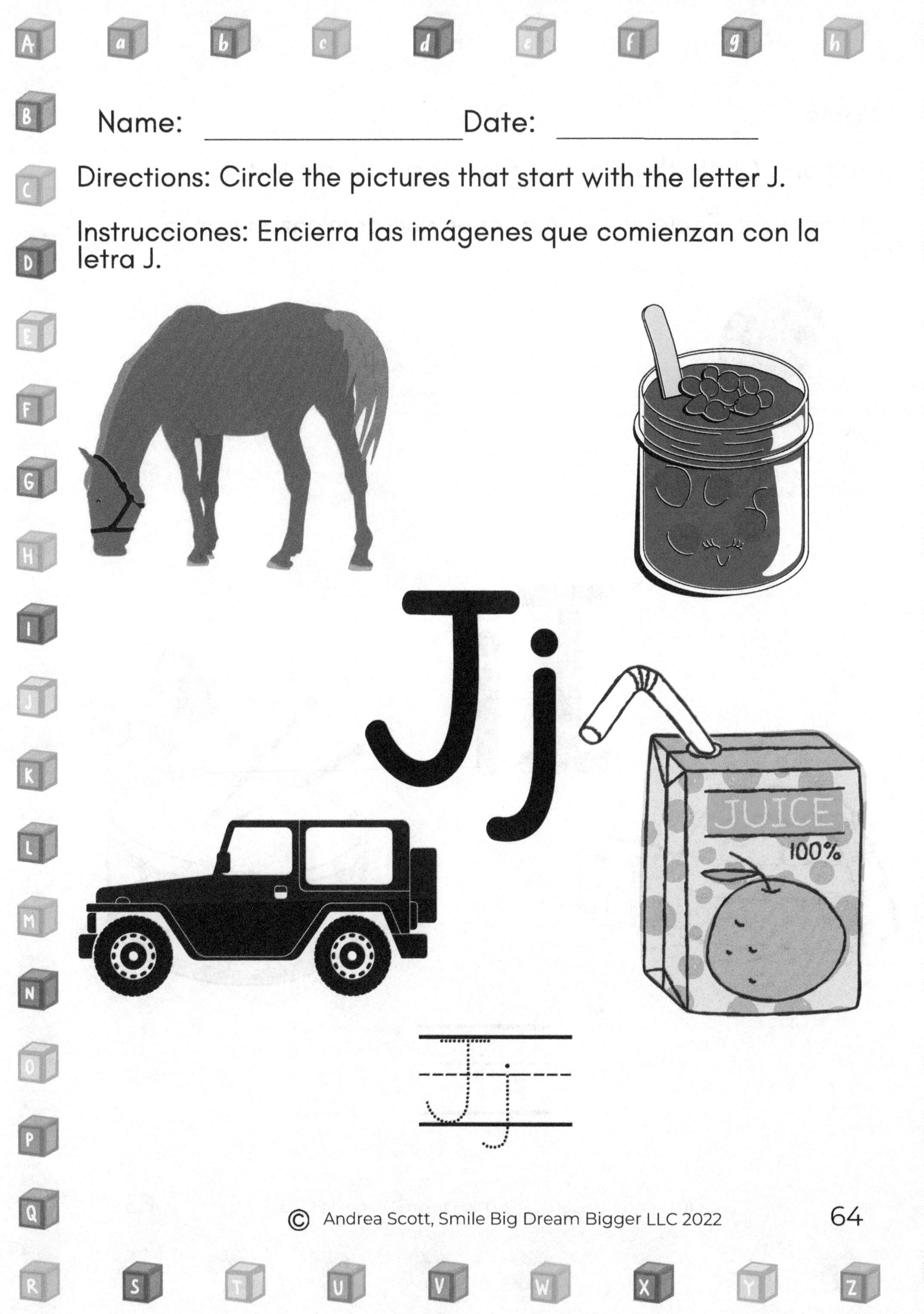

Name: ____________________ Date: ______________

Directions: Circle the pictures that start with the letter .K

Instrucciones: Encierra las imágenes que comienzan con la letra K.

Name: ____________________ Date: ______________

Directions: Circle the pictures that start with the letter L.

Instrucciones: Encierra las imágenes que comienzan con la letra L.

Name: ________________ Date: ____________

Directions: Circle the pictures that start with the letter M.

Instrucciones: Encierra las imágenes que comienzan con la letra M.

Name: ____________________ Date: ______________

Directions: Circle the pictures that start with the letter N

Instrucciones: Encierra las imágenes que comienzan con la letra N.

Name: ____________________ Date: ______________

Directions: Circle the pictures that start with the letter O.

Instrucciones: Encierra las imágenes que comienzan con la letra O.

Name: ____________________ Date: ______________

Directions: Circle the pictures that start with the letter P.

Instrucciones: Encierra las imágenes que comienzan con la letra P.

Pp

Name: ____________________ Date: ______________

Directions: Circle the pictures that start with the letter Q.

Instrucciones: Encierra las imágenes que comienzan con la letra Q.

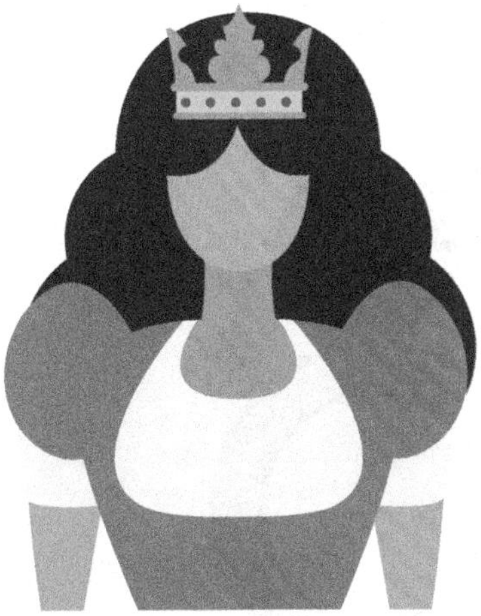

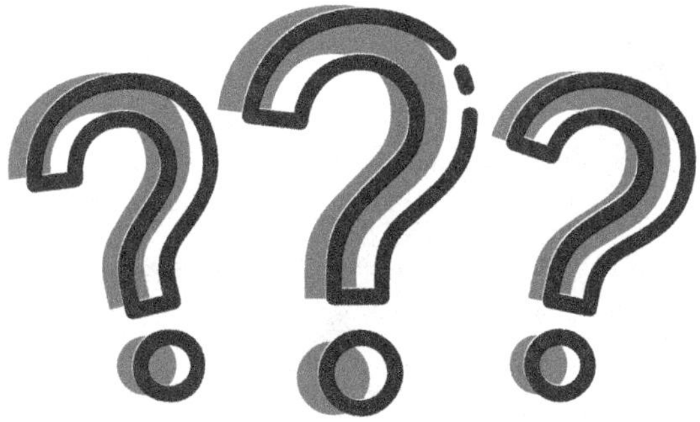

Qq

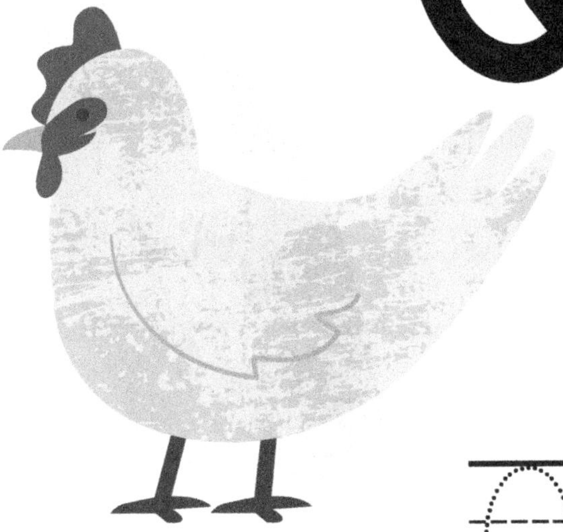

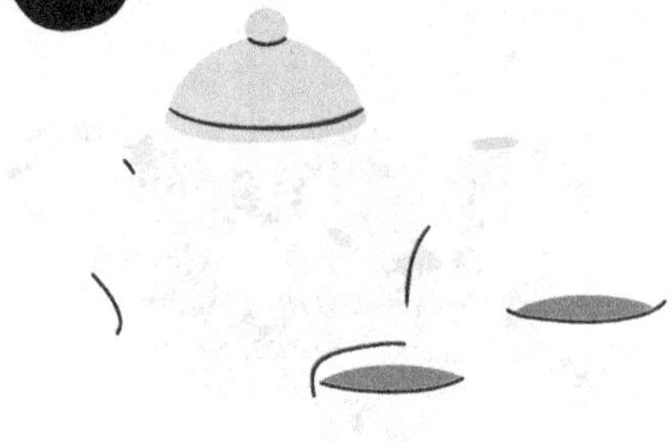

Qq

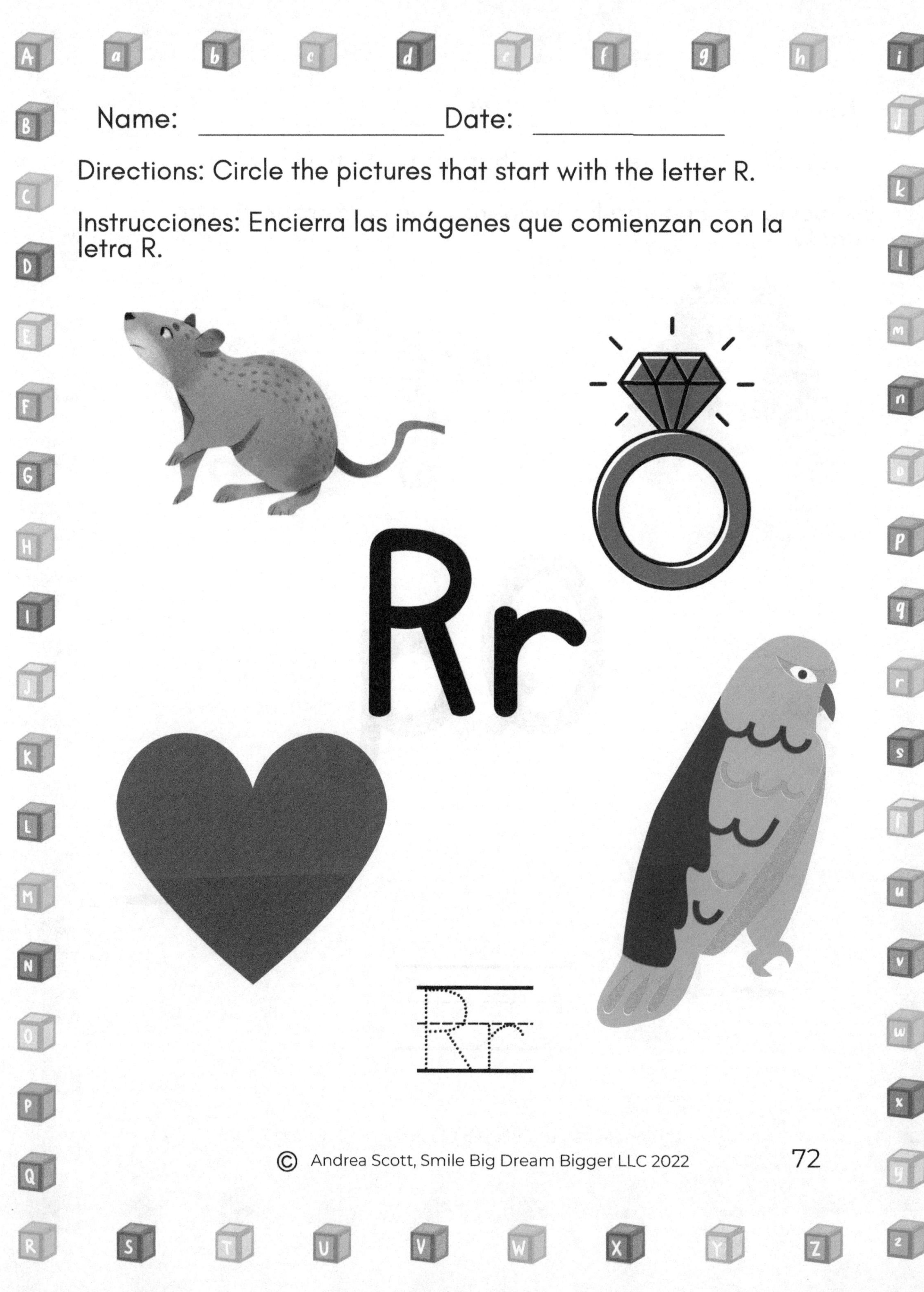

Name: ____________________ Date: ______________

Directions: Circle the pictures that start with the letter R.

Instrucciones: Encierra las imágenes que comienzan con la letra R.

Name: ____________________ Date: ______________

Directions: Circle the pictures that start with the letter S.

Instrucciones: Encierra las imágenes que comienzan con la letra S.

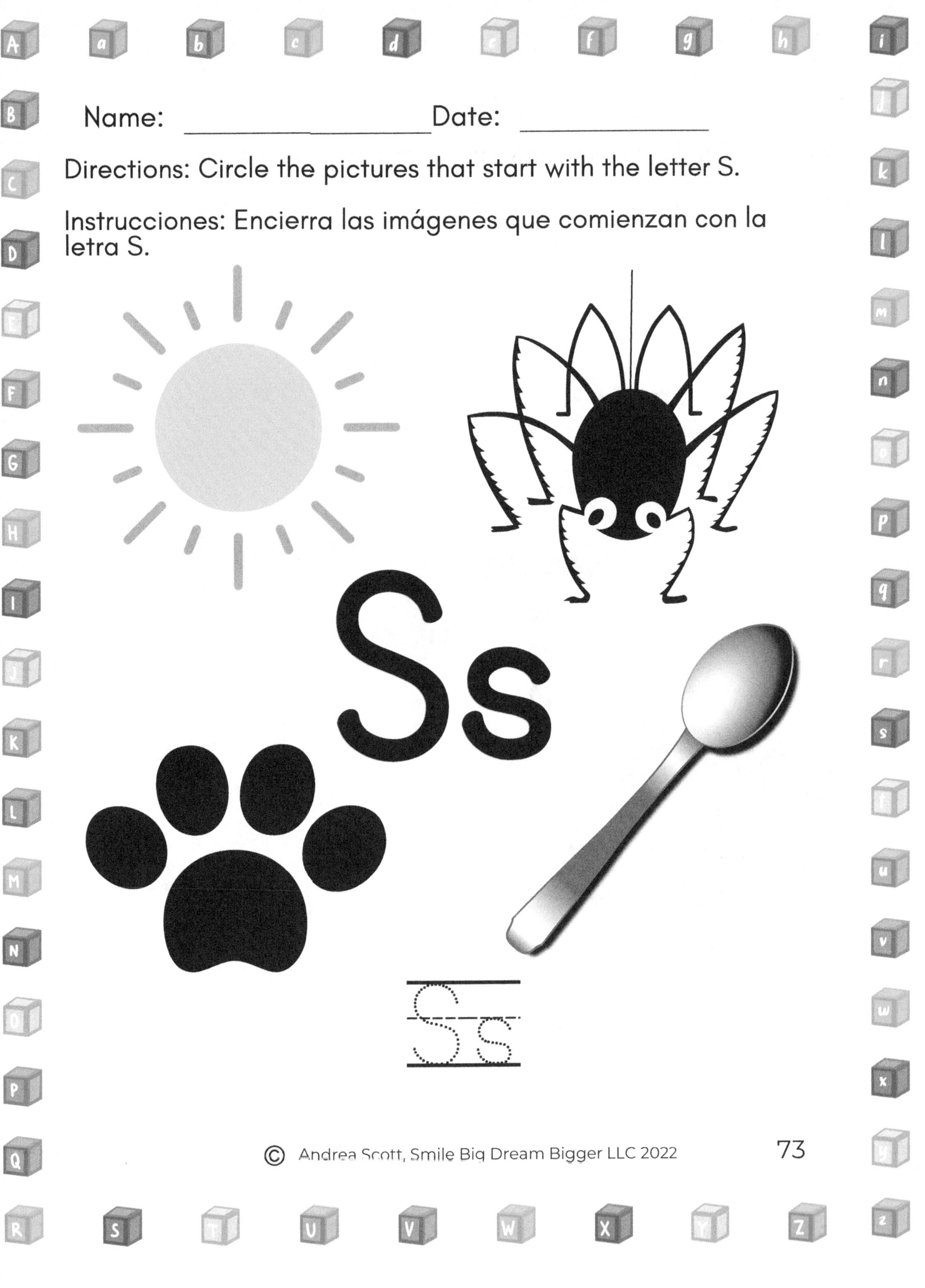

Name: ____________________ Date: ______________

Directions: Circle the pictures that start with the letter T.

Instrucciones: Encierra las imágenes que comienzan con la letra T.

Name: ____________________ Date: ______________

Directions: Circle the pictures that start with the letter U.

Instrucciones: Encierra las imágenes que comienzan con la letra U.

Uu

Name: ____________________ Date: ______________

Directions: Circle the pictures that start with the letter V.

Instrucciones: Encierra las imágenes que comienzan con la letra V.

Vv

Name: ____________________ Date: ______________

Directions: Circle the pictures that start with the letter W.

Instrucciones: Encierra las imágenes que comienzan con la letra W.

Ww

Ww

Name: ____________________ Date: ________________

Directions: Circle the pictures that start with the letter X.

Instrucciones: Encierra las imágenes que comienzan con la letra X.

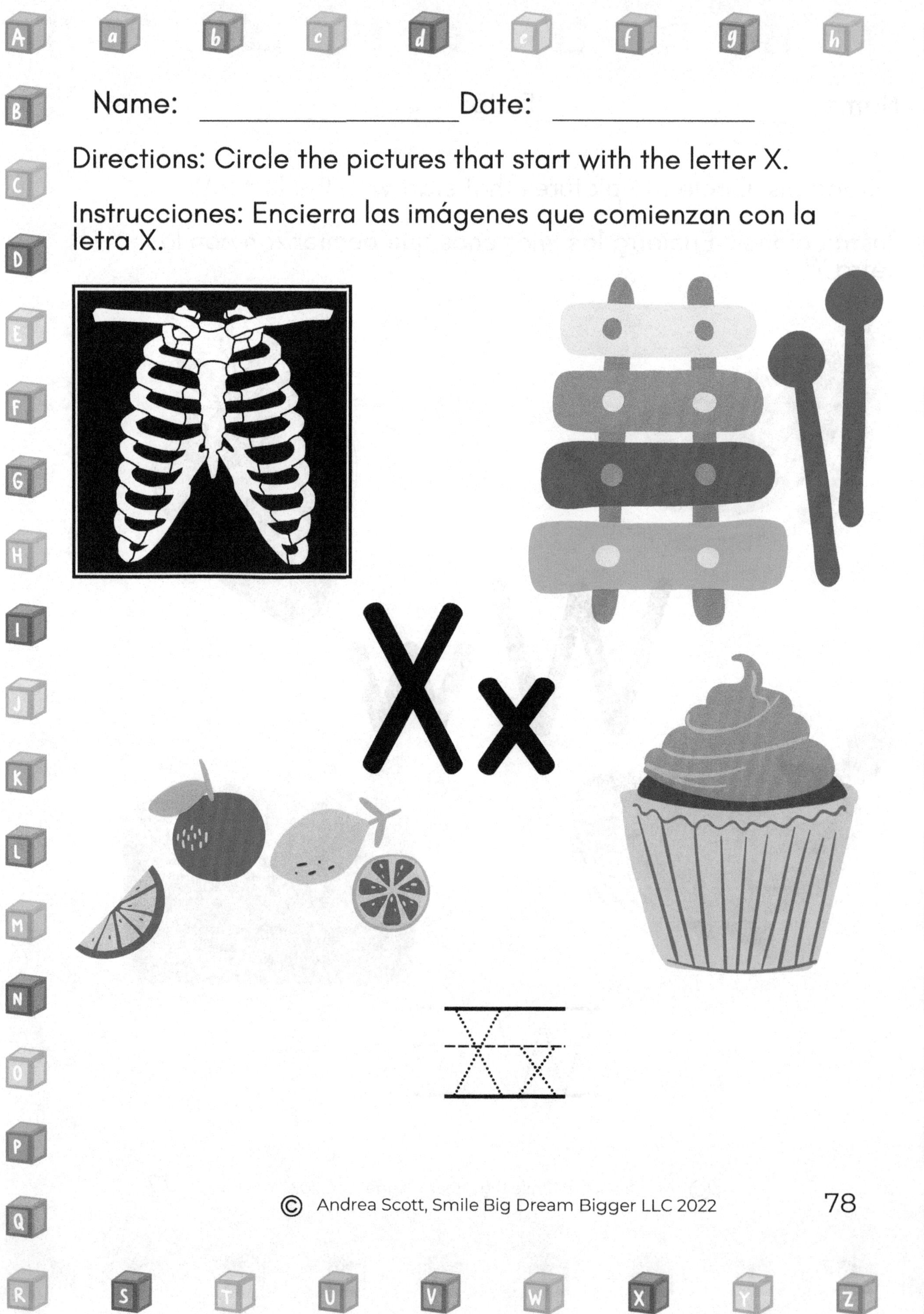

Name: ____________________ Date: ________________

Directions: Circle the pictures that start with the letter Y.

Instrucciones: Encierra las imágenes que comienzan con la letra Y.

Name: ________________ Date: ____________

Directions: Circle the pictures that start with the letter Z.

Instrucciones: Encierra las imágenes que comienzan con la letra Z.

Name: ____________________ Date: ______________

Directions: Practice tracing the uppercase and lowercase letters.

Instrucciones: Practique trazando letras mayúsculas y minúsculas.

Aa

Aa

Trace the bilingual words. Traza las palabras bilingües

airplane

avión

A a b c d e f g h i B j k l C D E F G H I J K L M N O P Q R S T U V W X Y Z m n o p q r s t u v w x y z

Name: ____________________ Date: ______________

Directions: Practice tracing the uppercase and lowercase letters.

Instrucciones: Practique trazando letras mayúsculas y minúsculas.

Bb

Bb

Trace the bilingual words. Traza las palabras bilingües

bicycle

bicicleta

Name: ____________________ Date: ______________

Directions: Practice tracing the uppercase and lowercase letters.

Instrucciones: Practique trazando letras mayúsculas y minúsculas.

Cc

Cc

Trace the bilingual words. Traza las palabras bilingües

cabin

cabina

Name: ____________________ Date: ________________

Directions: Practice tracing the uppercase and lowercase letters.

Instrucciones: Practique trazando letras mayúsculas y minúsculas.

Dd

Dd

Trace the bilingual words. Traza las palabras bilingües

dolphin

delfin

Name: ______________ Date: ____________

Directions: Practice tracing the uppercase and lowercase letters.

Instrucciones: Practique trazando letras mayúsculas y minúsculas.

Ee

Ee

Trace the bilingual words. Traza las palabras bilingües

elephant

elefante

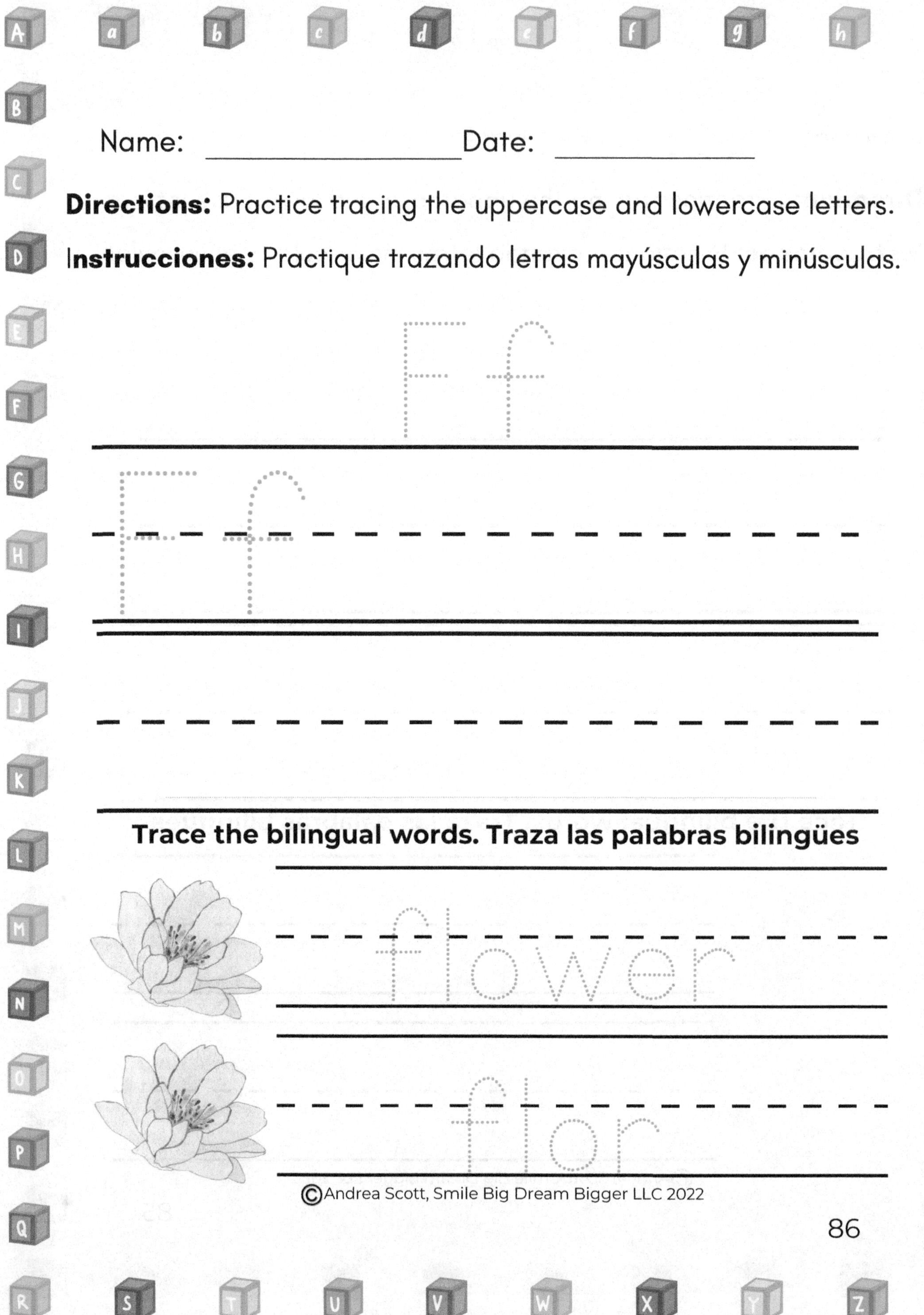

Name: ____________________ Date: ______________

Directions: Practice tracing the uppercase and lowercase letters.

Instrucciones: Practique trazando letras mayúsculas y minúsculas.

Ff

Ff

Trace the bilingual words. Traza las palabras bilingües

flower

flor

A a b c d e f g h i

Name: ________________ Date: ____________

Directions: Practice tracing the uppercase and lowercase letters.

Instrucciones: Practique trazando letras mayúsculas y minúsculas.

Gg

Gg

Trace the bilingual words. Traza las palabras bilingües

giant

gigante

Name: ____________________ Date: ______________

Directions: Practice tracing the uppercase and lowercase letters.

Instrucciones: Practique trazando letras mayúsculas y minúsculas.

Hh

Hh

Trace the bilingual words. Traza las palabras bilingües

hour

hora

Name: ____________________ Date: ______________

Directions: Practice tracing the uppercase and lowercase letters.

Instrucciones: Practique trazando letras mayúsculas y minúsculas.

Ii

Ii

Trace the bilingual words. Traza las palabras bilingües

iguana

iguana

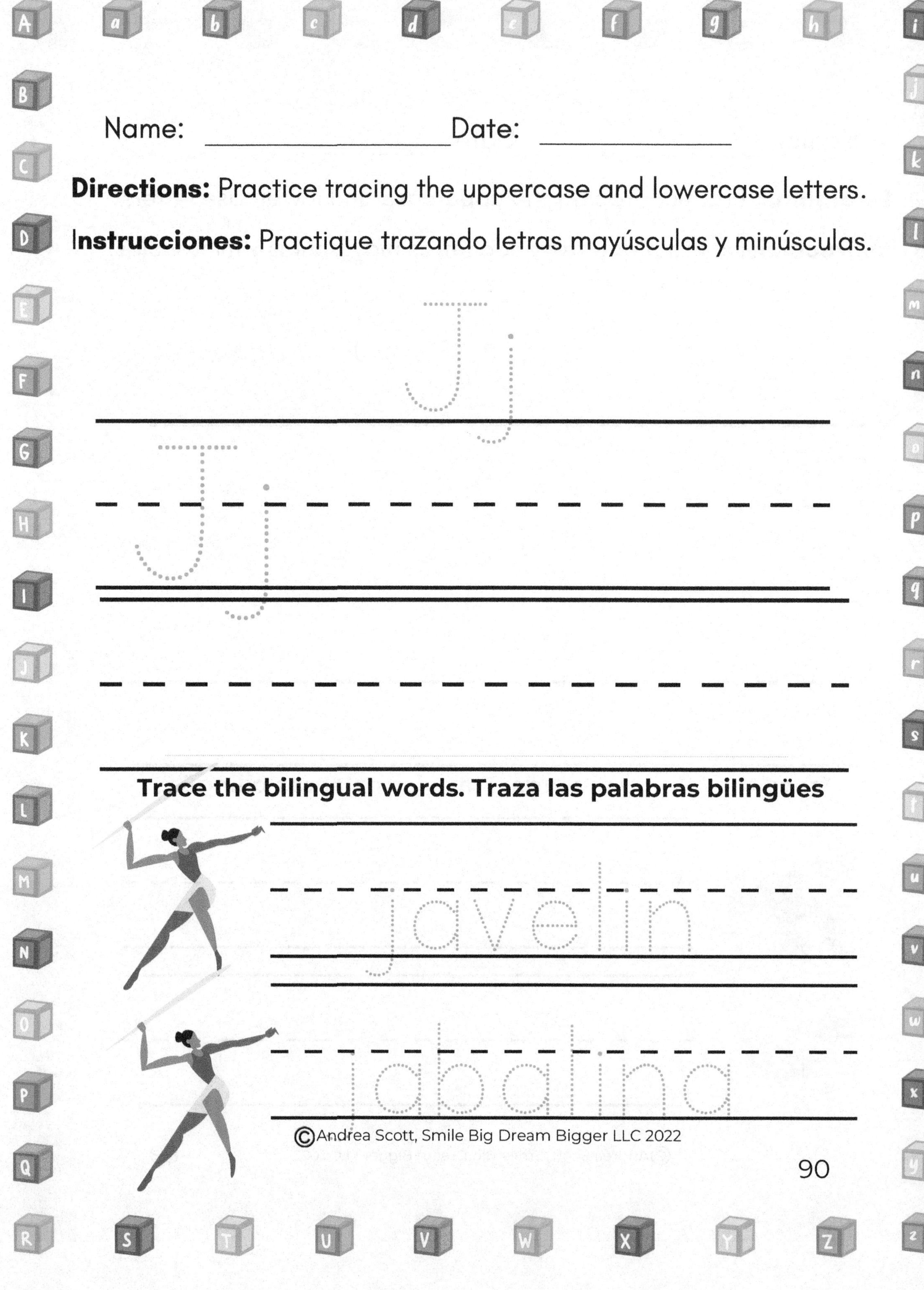

Name: ________________ Date: ____________

Directions: Practice tracing the uppercase and lowercase letters.

Instrucciones: Practique trazando letras mayúsculas y minúsculas.

Jj

Jj

Trace the bilingual words. Traza las palabras bilingües

javelin

jabalina

Name: ______________ Date: __________

Directions: Practice tracing the uppercase and lowercase letters.

Instrucciones: Practique trazando letras mayúsculas y minúsculas.

Kk

Kk

Trace the bilingual words. Traza las palabras bilingües

koala

koala

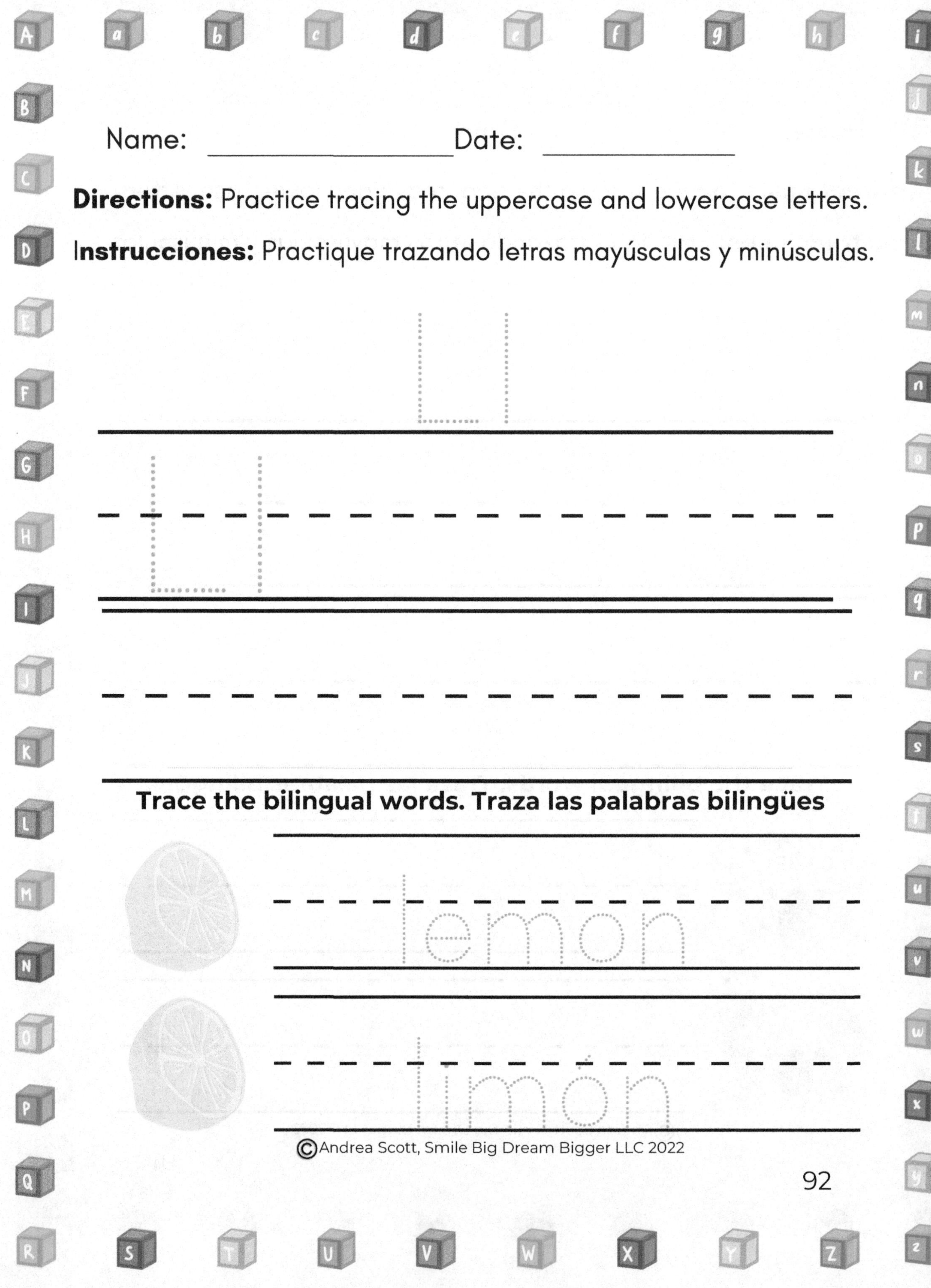

Name: ____________________ Date: ______________

Directions: Practice tracing the uppercase and lowercase letters.

Instrucciones: Practique trazando letras mayúsculas y minúsculas.

Ll

Ll

Trace the bilingual words. Traza las palabras bilingües

lemon

limón

Name: ________________ Date: ____________

Directions: Practice tracing the uppercase and lowercase letters.

Instrucciones: Practique trazando letras mayúsculas y minúsculas.

Mm

Mm

Trace the bilingual words. Traza las palabras bilingües

map

mapa

Name: ____________________ Date: ______________

Directions: Practice tracing the uppercase and lowercase letters.

Instrucciones: Practique trazando letras mayúsculas y minúsculas.

Nn

Nn

Trace the bilingual words. Traza las palabras bilingües

nose

nariz

Name: ________________ Date: ____________

Directions: Practice tracing the uppercase and lowercase letters.

I**nstrucciones:** Practique trazando letras mayúsculas y minúsculas.

Oo

Oo

Trace the bilingual words. Traza las palabras bilingües

office

oficina

A a b c d e f g h i

B j

Name: ____________________ Date: ______________

C k

Directions: Practice tracing the uppercase and lowercase letters.

Instrucciones: Practique trazando letras mayúsculas y minúsculas.

D l

E m

Pp

F n

G o

Pp

H p

I q

J r

K s

L t

Trace the bilingual words. Traza las palabras bilingües

M u

POPCORN

N v

popcorn

O w

POPCORN

P x

palomitas

Q y

R S T U V W X Y Z z

Name: ________________ Date: ____________

Directions: Practice tracing the uppercase and lowercase letters.

Instrucciones: Practique trazando letras mayúsculas y minúsculas.

Qq

Qq

Trace the bilingual words. Traza las palabras bilingües

quesadilla

quesadilla

Name: ____________________ Date: ______________

Directions: Practice tracing the uppercase and lowercase letters.

Instrucciones: Practique trazando letras mayúsculas y minúsculas.

Rr

Rr

Trace the bilingual words. Traza las palabras bilingües

rose

rosa

Name: ____________________ Date: ______________

Directions: Practice tracing the uppercase and lowercase letters.

Instrucciones: Practique trazando letras mayúsculas y minúsculas.

Ss

Ss

Trace the bilingual words. Traza las palabras bilingües

sun

sol

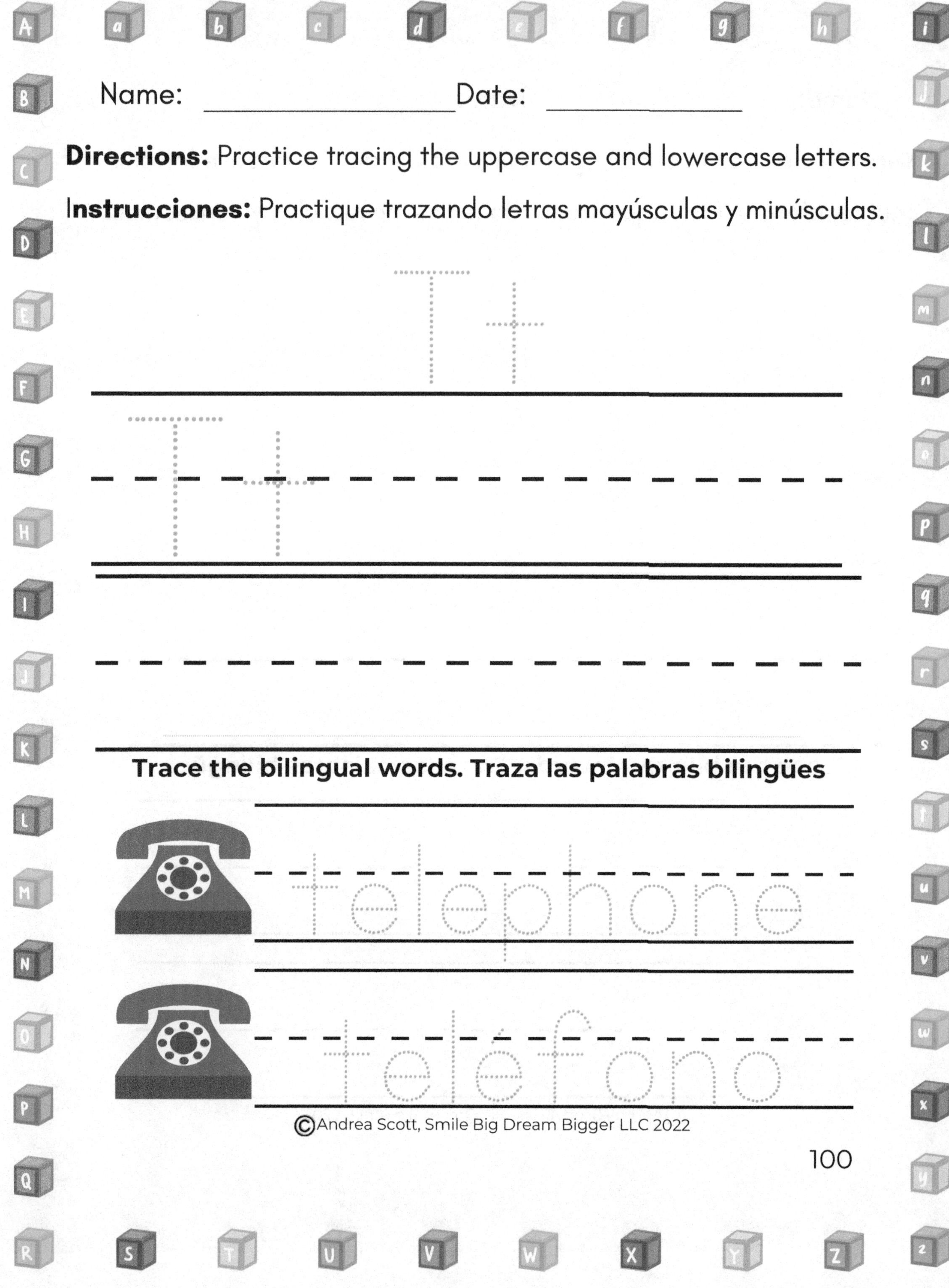

Name: ____________________ Date: ______________

Directions: Practice tracing the uppercase and lowercase letters.

Instrucciones: Practique trazando letras mayúsculas y minúsculas.

Tt

Tt

Trace the bilingual words. Traza las palabras bilingües

telephone

teléfono

Name: ____________________ Date: ______________

Directions: Practice tracing the uppercase and lowercase letters.

Instrucciones: Practique trazando letras mayúsculas y minúsculas.

Uu

Uu

Trace the bilingual words. Traza las palabras bilingües

unity

unidad

Name: ____________________ Date: ________________

Directions: Practice tracing the uppercase and lowercase letters.

Instrucciones: Practique trazando letras mayúsculas y minúsculas.

V v

V v

Trace the bilingual words. Traza las palabras bilingües

voice

voz

Name: ____________________ Date: ______________

Directions: Practice tracing the uppercase and lowercase letters.

Instrucciones: Practique trazando letras mayúsculas y minúsculas.

Ww

Ww

Trace the bilingual words. Traza las palabras bilingües

Wi-Fi

Wi-fi

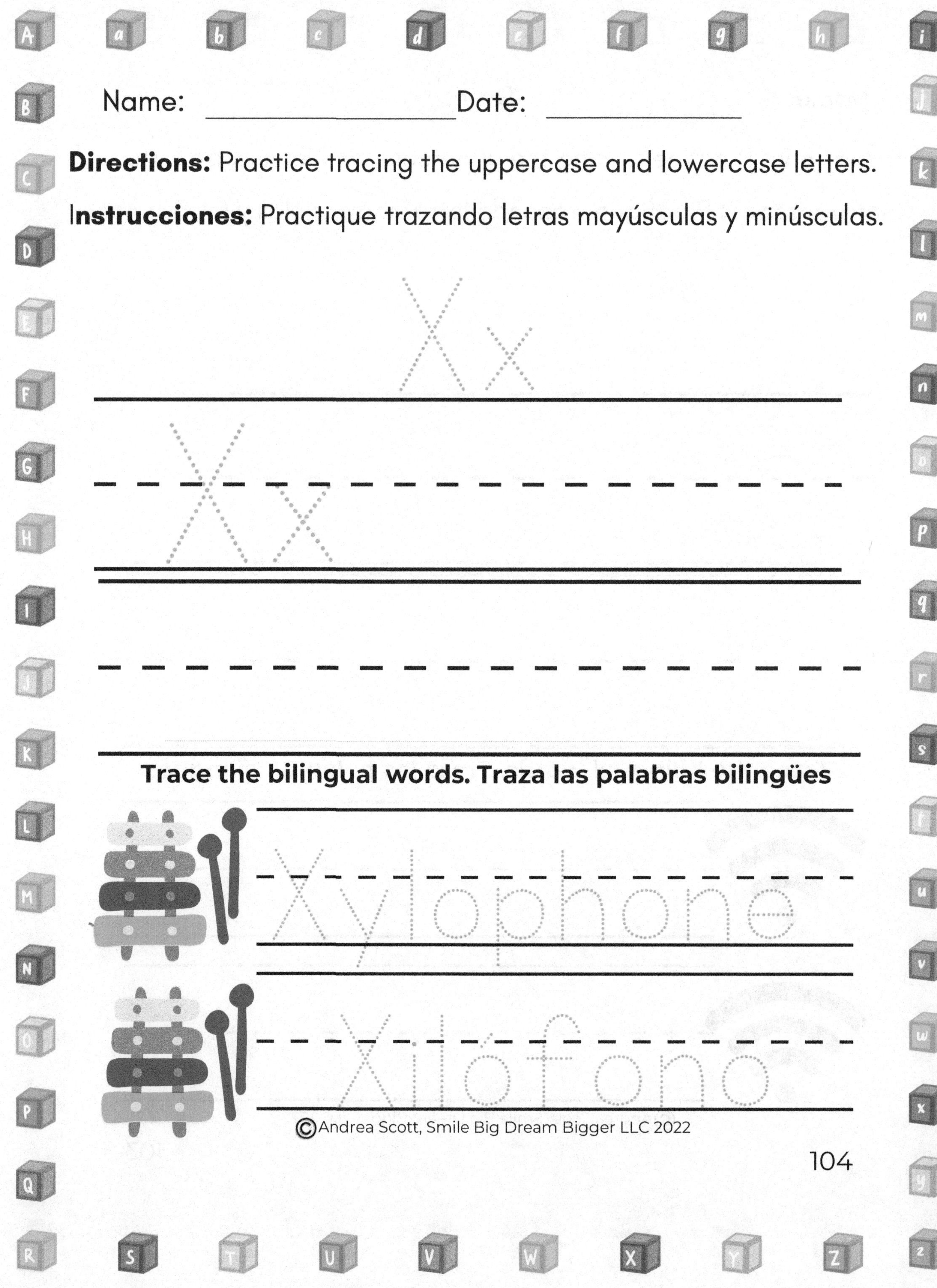

Name: ____________________ Date: ________________

Directions: Practice tracing the uppercase and lowercase letters.

Instrucciones: Practique trazando letras mayúsculas y minúsculas.

Xx

Xx

Trace the bilingual words. Traza las palabras bilingües

Xylophone

Xilófono

Name: ____________________ Date: ______________

Directions: Practice tracing the uppercase and lowercase letters.

Instrucciones: Practique trazando letras mayúsculas y minúsculas.

Yy

Yy

Trace the bilingual words. Traza las palabras bilingües

yolk

yema

A a b c d e f g h i

B Name: ____________ Date: ____________ j

Directions: Practice tracing the uppercase and lowercase letters.

Instrucciones: Practique trazando letras mayúsculas y minúsculas.

Zz

Zz

Trace the bilingual words. Traza las palabras bilingües

zone

zona

R S T U V W X Y Z z

Name: ____________________ Date: ______________

Trace/Trazar:

A a A a A a A a

A a A a A a A a

Write/Escribir:

A

a

Name: ____________________ Date: ______________

Trace/Trazar:

B b B b B b B b

B b B b B b B b

Write/Escribir:

B

b

Name: ____________________ Date: ______________

Trace/Trazar:

Write/Escribir:

Name: ____________________ Date: __________________

Trace/Trazar:

Dd Dd Dd Dd

Dd Dd Dd Dd

Write/Escribir:

D

d

Name: ____________________ Date: ________________

Trace/Trazar:

E e E e E e E e

E e E e E e E e

Write/Escribir:

E

e

Name: ____________________ Date: __________________

Trace/Trazar:

Write/Escribir:

Name: ____________________ Date: __________________

Trace/Trazar:

Gg Gg Gg Gg

Gg Gg Gg Gg

Write/Escribir:

G

g

Name: ____________________ Date: ____________________

Trace/Trazar:

Write/Escribir:

Name: ____________________ Date: __________________

Trace/Trazar:

I i I i I i I i I i I i

I i I i I i I i I i I i

Write/Escribir:

I

i

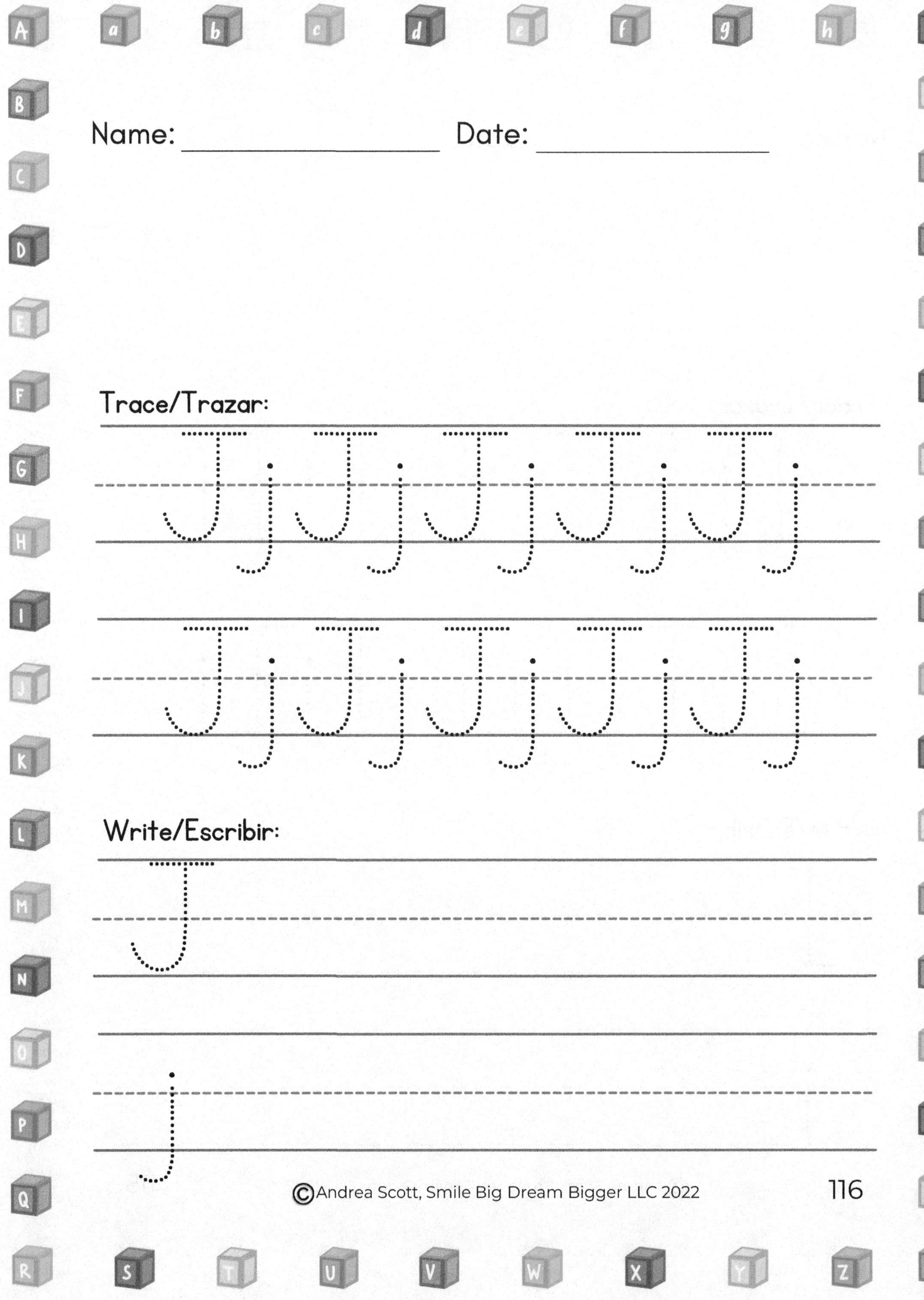

Name: ________________ Date: ________________

Trace/Trazar:

Write/Escribir:

Name: ____________________ Date: ________________

Trace/Trazar:

K k K k K k K k

K k K k K k K k

Write/Escribir:

K

k

Name: ____________________ Date: ____________________

Trace/Trazar:

Write/Escribir:

Name: ____________________ Date: __________________

Trace/Trazar:

M m M m M m

M m M m M m

Write/Escribir:

M

m

Name: ________________ Date: ________________

Trace/Trazar:

Nn Nn Nn Nn

Nn Nn Nn Nn

Write/Escribir:

N

n

Name: ____________________ Date: __________________

Trace/Trazar:

O o O o O o O o

O o O o O o O o

Write/Escribir:

O

o

Name:
Date:
Trace/Trazar:
Write/Escribir:

Name: ________________ Date: ______________

Trace/Trazar:

Qq Qq Qq Qq

Qq Qq Qq Qq

Write/Escribir:

Q

q

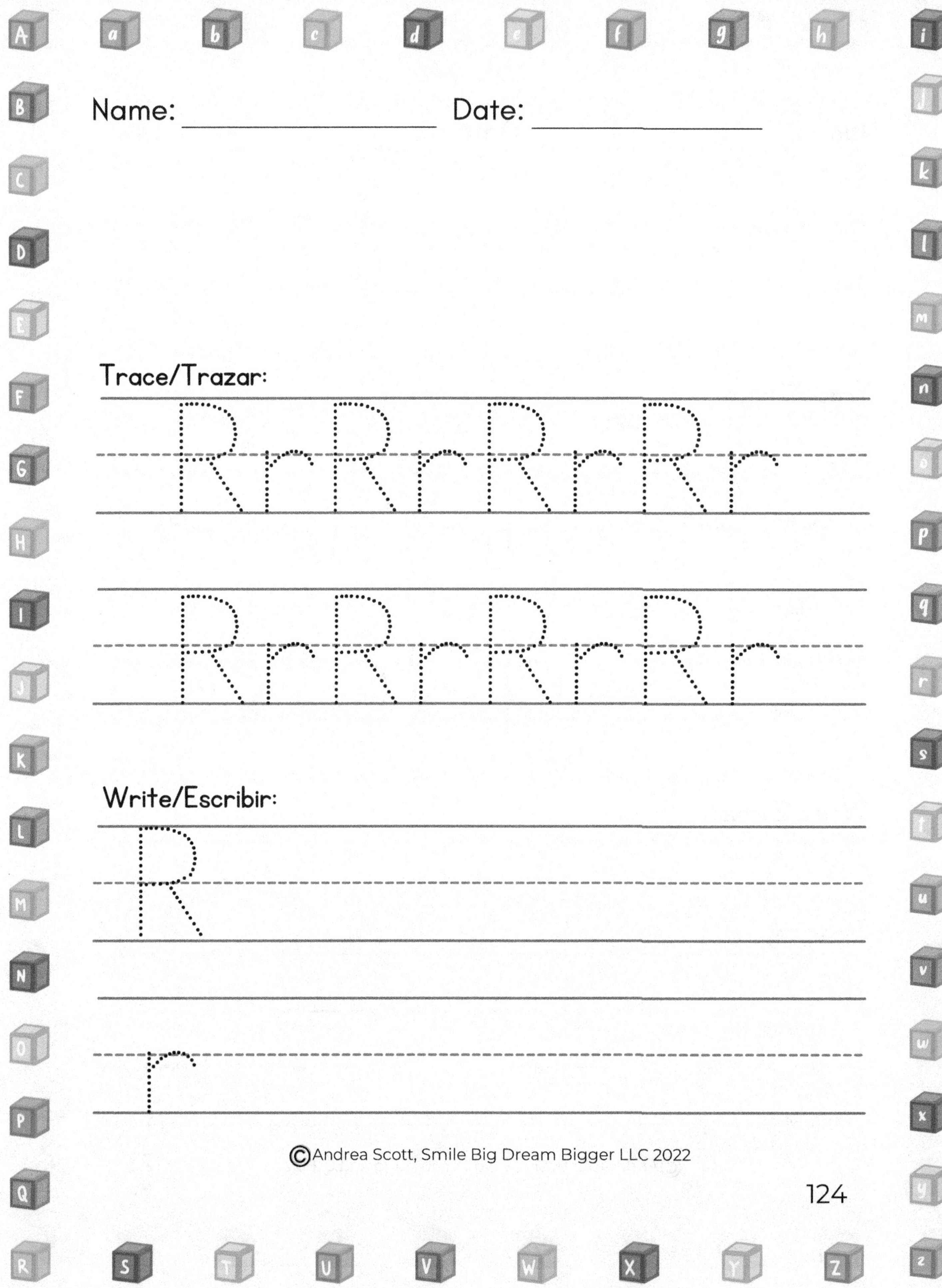

Name: ____________________ Date: __________________

Trace/Trazar:

Rr Rr Rr Rr

Rr Rr Rr Rr

Write/Escribir:

R

r

Name: ____________________ Date: __________________

Trace/Trazar:

S s S s S s S s

S s S s S s S s

Write/Escribir:

S

s

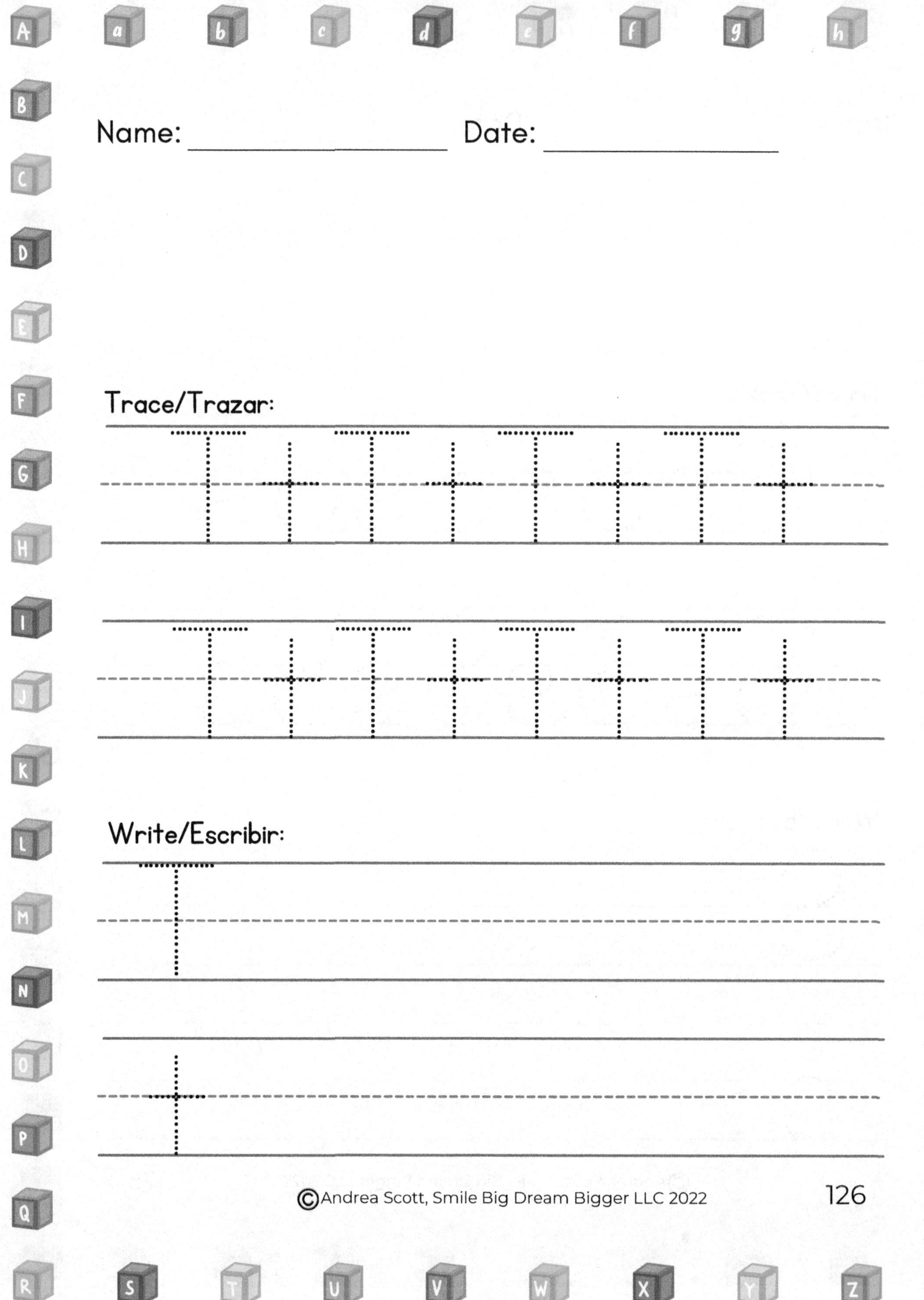

Name: ____________________ Date: __________________

Trace/Trazar:

Write/Escribir:

Name: ____________________ Date: __________________

Trace/Trazar:

Write/Escribir:

Name: ____________________ Date: __________________

Trace/Trazar:

Write/Escribir:

Name: ________________ Date: ______________

Trace/Trazar:

W w W w W w

W w W w W w

Write/Escribir:

W

w

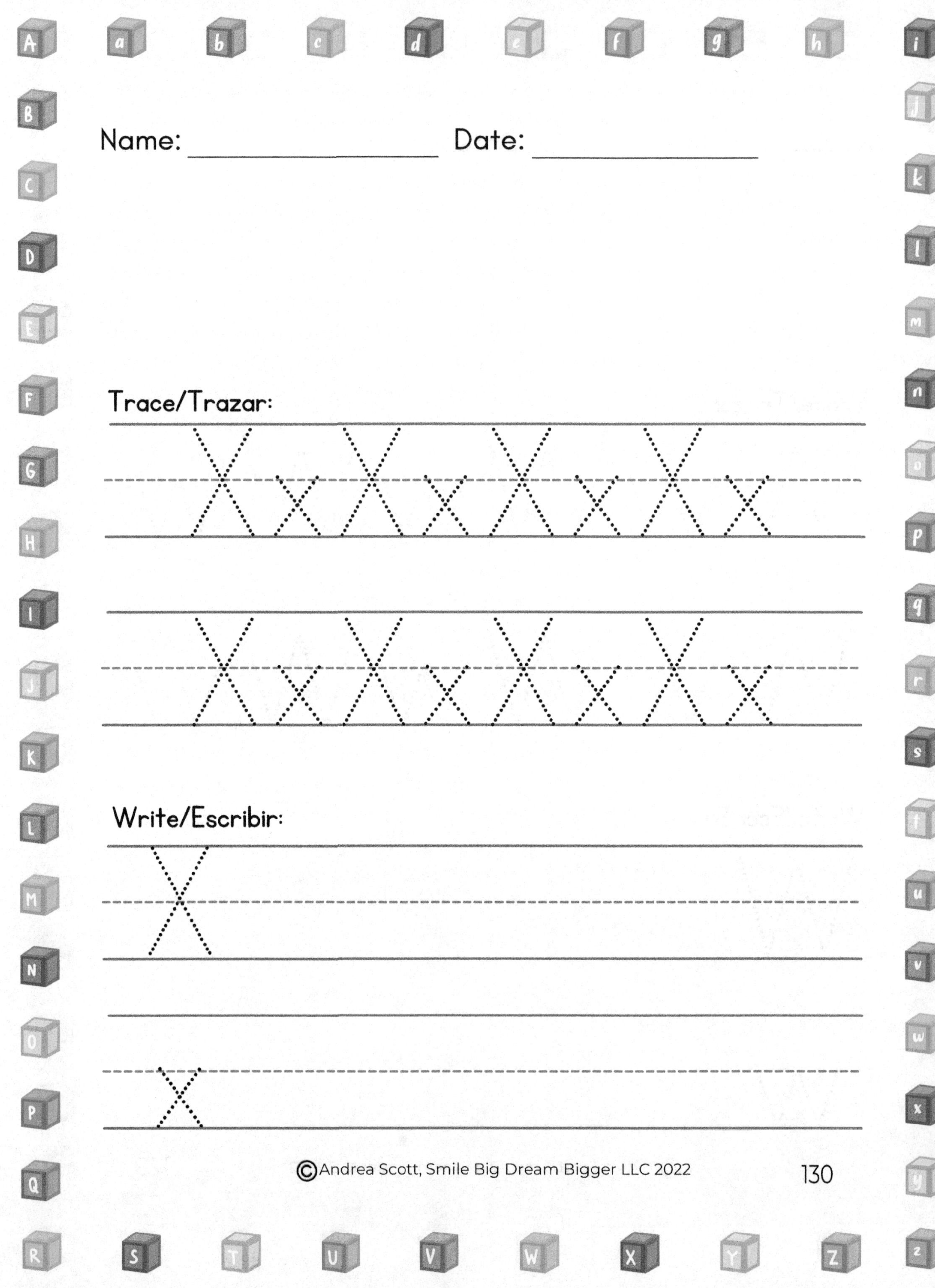

Name:
Date:
Trace/Trazar:
Write/Escribir:

Name: ________________ Date: ______________

Trace/Trazar:

Yy Yy Yy Yy

Yy Yy Yy Yy

Write/Escribir:

Y

y

Name: ____________________ Date: __________________

Trace/Trazar:

Write/Escribir:

Name:_______________ Date:___________

Directions: Color the picture
Instrucciones: Colorea el dibujo

A a b c d e f g h i

B j

Name:_______________ Date:___________

C k

Directions: Color the picture
Instrucciones: Colorea el dibujo

D l E m F n G o H p I q J r K s L t M u N v O w P x Q y

R S T U V W X Y Z z

Name:_________________ Date:_____________

Directions: Color the picture
Instrucciones: Colorea el dibujo

Name:__________________ Date:______________

Directions: Color the picture
Instrucciones: Colorea el dibujo

Name:________________ Date:____________

Directions: Color the picture
Instrucciones: Colorea el dibujo

Name:_________________ Date:_____________

Directions: Color the picture
Instrucciones: Colorea el dibujo

Name:_______________ Date:____________

Directions: Color the picture
Instrucciones: Colorea el dibujo

Bilingual Primary Colors

Green/Verde

Blue/Azul

Rojo/Red

Morado

Naranja/Orange

Name: ___________________________
Directions:
1. Circle the green objects.
2. Color the word green.
3. Choose the green crayon and color the blank images.
Green

Nombre: ______________________________

Instrucciones:
1. Encierra en un círculo el objeto verde.
2. Colorea la palabra verde.
3. Selecciona el lápiz de color verde, luego colorea los imagenes blancos.

Name: ______________________________

Directions:
1. Circle the blue objects.
2. Color the word blue.
3. Choose the blue crayon and color the blank images.

Blue

Nombre: ____________________________

Instrucciones:

1. Encierra en un círculo el objeto azul.
2. Colorea la palabra azul.
3. Selecciona el lapiz de color azul, luego colorea las imagenes blancas.

Name: ______________________________

Directions:

1. Circle the yellow objects.
2. Color the word yellow.
3. Choose the yellow crayon and color the blank images.

Nombre: ____________________________

Instrucciones:
1. Encierra en un círculo el objeto amarillo.
2. Colorea la palabra "amarillo."
3. Selecciona el lápiz de color amarillo, luego colorea las imagenes blancas.

Name:
Directions:
1. Circle the red objects.
2. Color the word "red".
3. Choose the red crayon and color the blank images.
STOP
Red

Nombre: ___________________________

Instrucciones:

1. Encierra en un círculo el objeto rojo.
2. Colorea la palabra "rojo".
3. Selecciona el lapiz de color rojo, luego colorea las imágenes blancas.

Name: ______________________________

Directions:

1. Circle the purple images.
2. Color the word "purple".
3. Choose the purple crayon, then color the blank images.

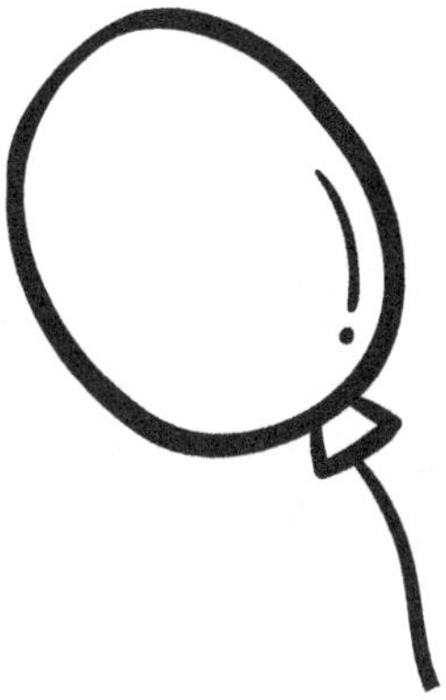

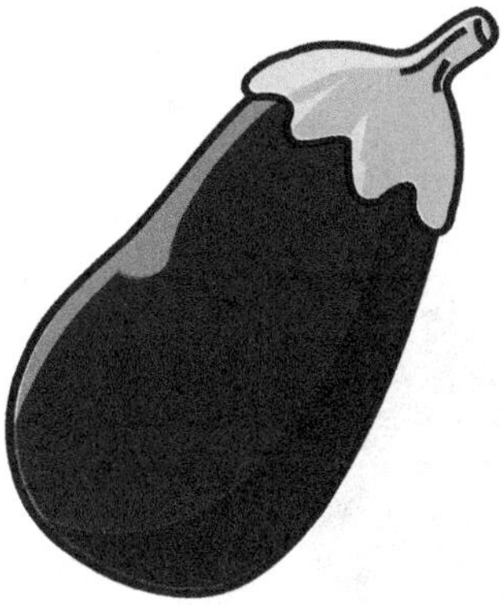

Purple

Nombre: ____________________________

Instrucciones:

1. Encierra en un círculo el objeto morado.
2. Colorea la palabra "morado".
3. Selecciona el lápiz de color morado, luego colorea las imágenes blancas.

Name: ______________________________

Directions:

1. Circle the orange images.
2. Color the word "orange ".
3. Choose the orange crayon, then color the blank images.

Orange

Nombre: ______________________
Instrucciones:
1. Encierra en un círculo el objeto anaranjado.
2. Colorea la palabra "anaranjado".
3. Selecciona el lapiz de color anarajado, luego colorea las imágenes blancas.
Anaranjado

Name: ______________________________

Directions:

1. Circle the gray images.
2. Color the word "gray".
3. Choose the gray crayon, then color the blank images.

Gray

Nombre: ______________________________

Instrucciones:

1. Encierra en un círculo el objeto gris.
2. Colorea la palabra "gris".
3. Selecciona el lápiz de color gris, luego colorea las imágenes blancas.

Name: ______________________________

Directions:

1. Circle the black images.
2. Color the word "black".
3. Choose the black crayon, then color the blank images.

Black

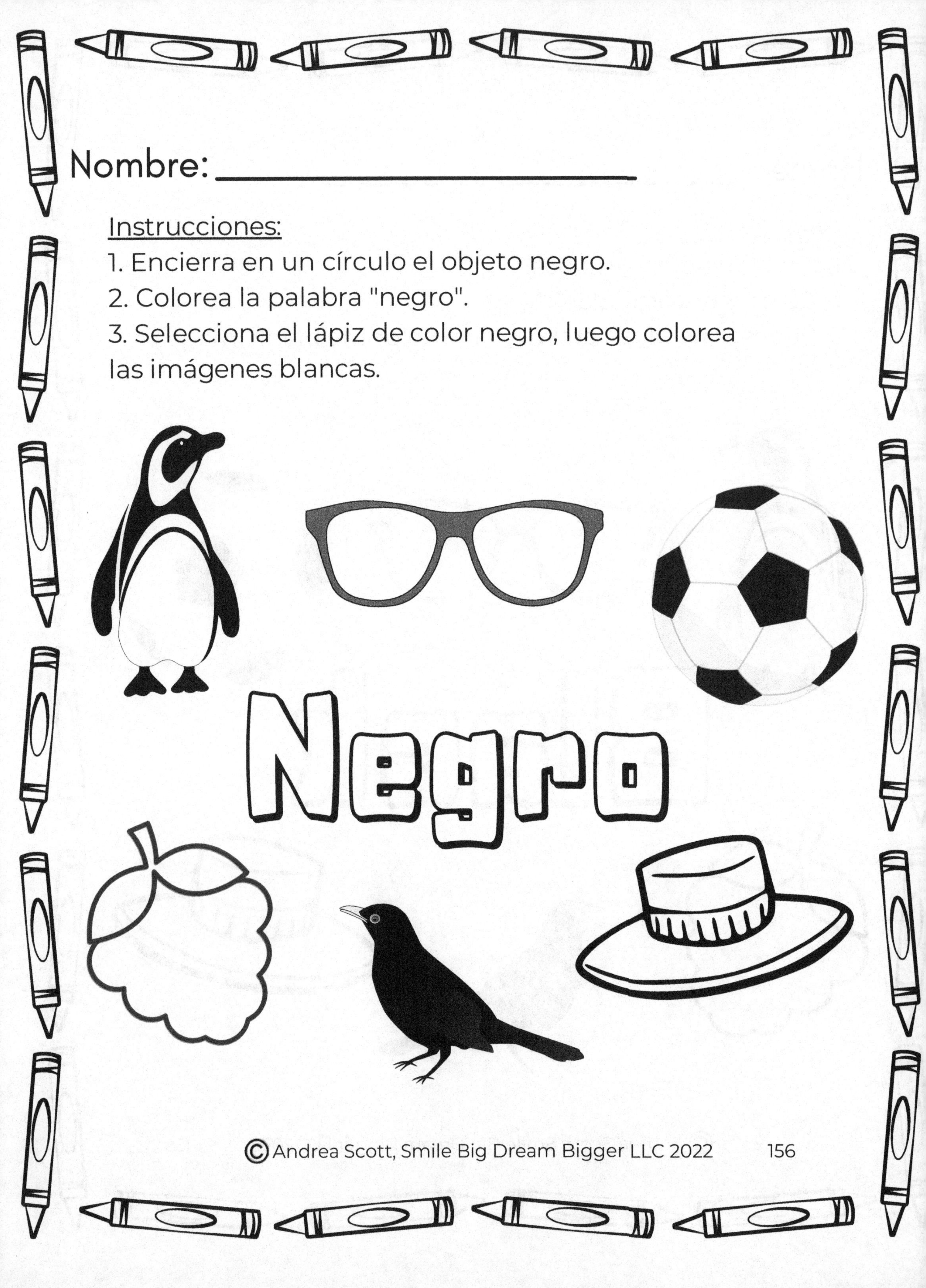
Nombre: ___________________________

Instrucciones:
1. Encierra en un círculo el objeto negro.
2. Colorea la palabra "negro".
3. Selecciona el lápiz de color negro, luego colorea las imágenes blancas.

Negro

Name: ______________________________

Directions:

1. Circle the brown images.
2. Color the word "brown".
3. Choose the brown crayon, then color the blank images.

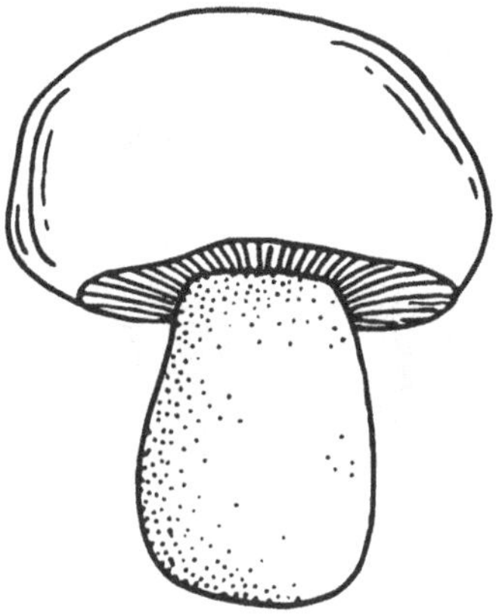

Brown

Nombre: ______________________________

Instrucciones:

1. Encierra en un círculo el objeto marrón.
2. Colorea la palabra "marrón".
3. Selecciona el lápiz de color marrón, luego colorea las imágenes blancas.

Name: ______________________

Directions:

1. Circle the pink images.
2. Color the word "pink".
3. Choose the pink crayon, then color the blank images.

Pink

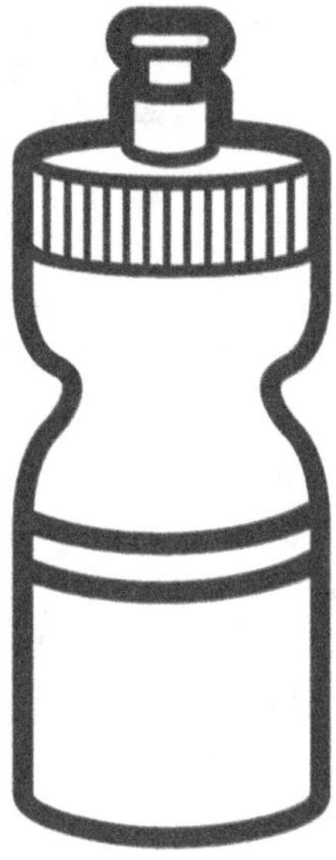

Nombre: ____________________________

Instrucciones:

1. Encierra en un círculo el objeto rosado.
2. Colorea la palabra "rosado"
3. Selecciona el lápiz de color rosado, luego colorea las imágenes blancas.

Name: ____________________ Date: ______________

Directions: Draw a line that connects each crayon to line with the corresponding color.

Instrucciones: Dibuje una linea que conecta cada marcador con el color que corresponde.

Azul

Rojo

Morado

Verde

Amarillo

Anaranjado

Negro

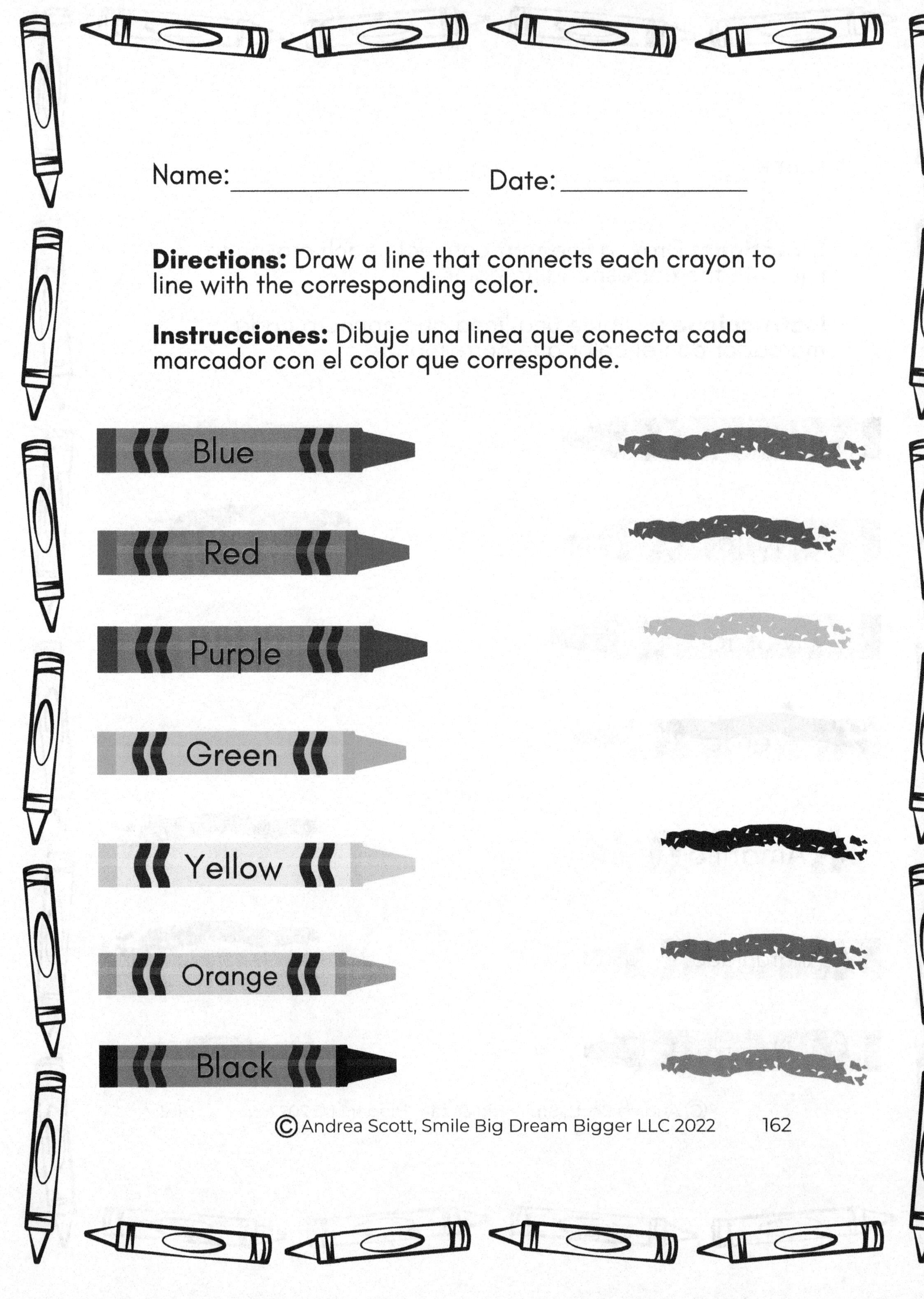

Name: ____________________ Date: ________________

Directions: Draw a line that connects each crayon to line with the corresponding color.

Instrucciones: Dibuje una linea que conecta cada marcador con el color que corresponde.

Name:____________________ Date:______________

Directions: Color the crayon with the corresponding color.

Instrucciones: Colorea el marcador con el color que corresponde.

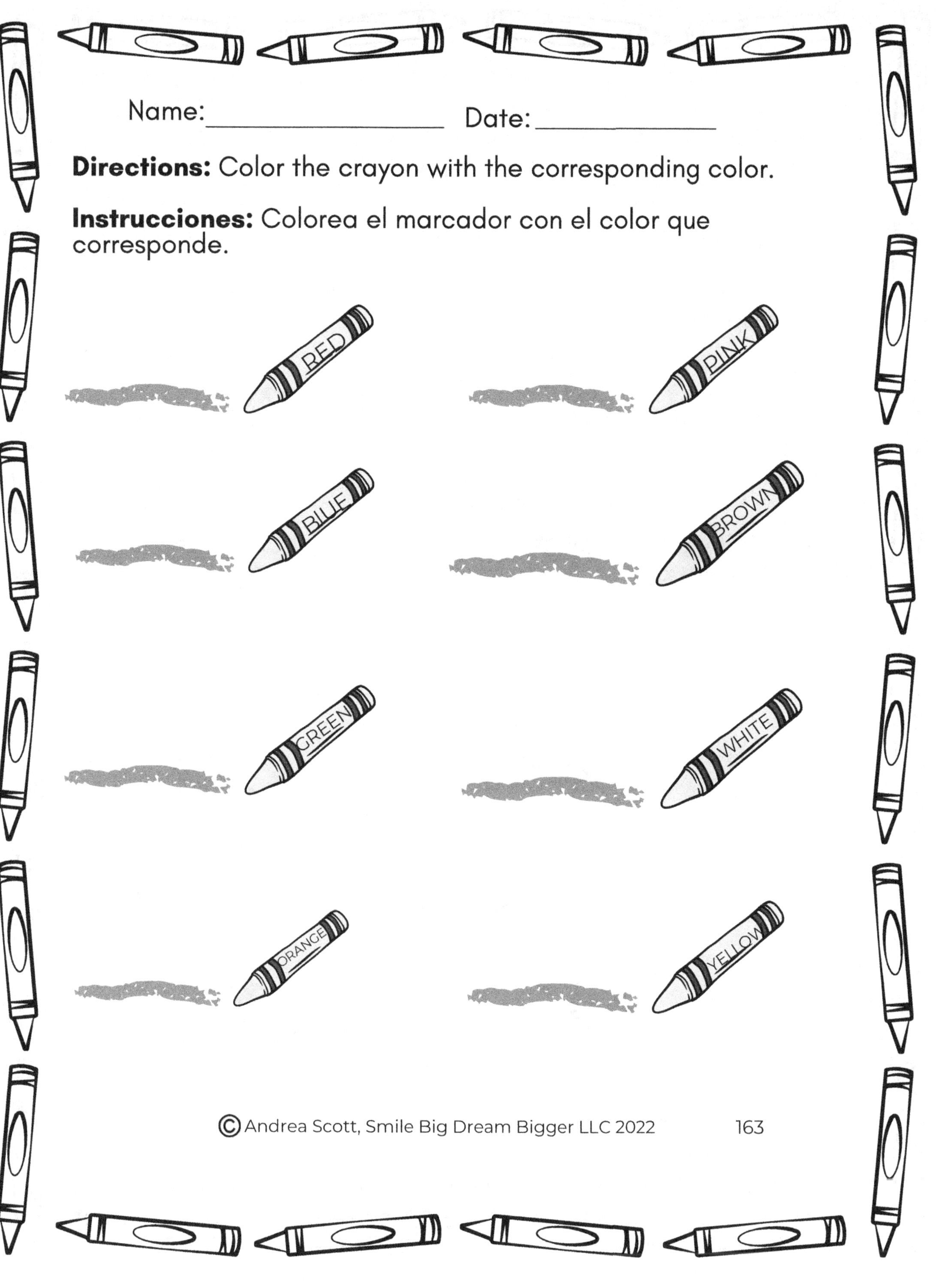

Name:_______________ Date:_____________

Directions: Color the crayon with the corresponding color.

Instrucciones: Colorea el marcador con el color que corresponde.

ROJO

ROSADO

AZUL

MARRON

VERDE

BLANCO

ANARANJADO

AMARILLO

Name:__________________ Date:______________
Colorful Afros
Directions: Color each box with the corresponding color to its afro.
Instrucciones: Colorea cada caja con el color que corresponde con el afro.
Green
Red
Black
Blue
Yellow

Name:__________________ Date:______________

Colorful Afros

Directions: Color each box with the corresponding color to its afro.
Instrucciones: Colorea cada caja con el color que corresponde con el afro.

Name:________________ Date:______________

Colorful Afros

Directions: Color each box with the corresponding color to its afro.
Instrucciones: Colorea cada caja con el color que corresponde con el afro.

Rosado

Amarillo

Negro

Azul

Verde

Name:________________ Date:____________

Colorful Afros

Directions: Color each box with the corresponding color to its afro.
Instrucciones: Colorea cada caja con el color que corresponde con el afro.

Shapes/Figuras

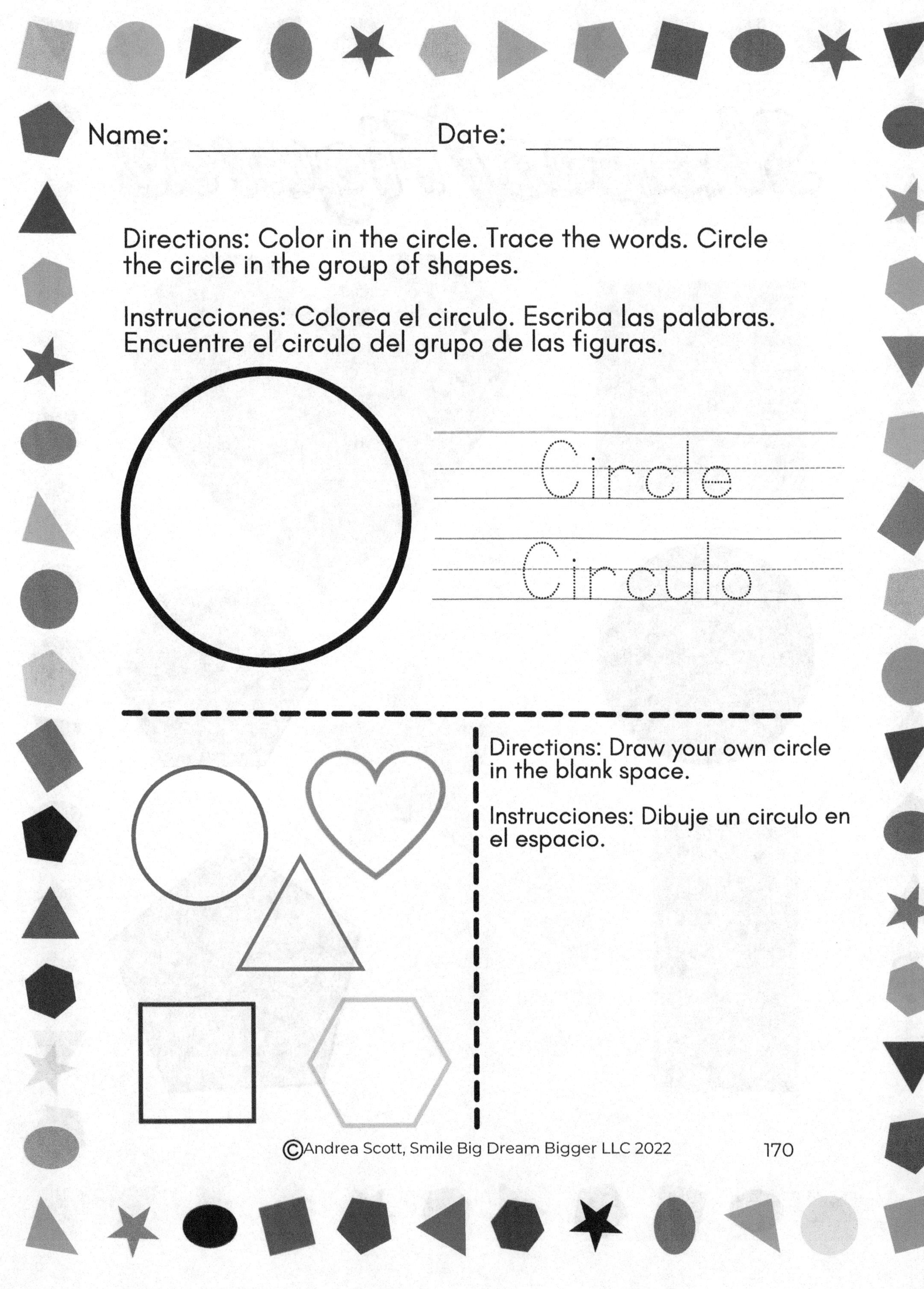

Name: ________________ Date: ____________

Directions: Color in the circle. Trace the words. Circle the circle in the group of shapes.

Instrucciones: Colorea el circulo. Escriba las palabras. Encuentre el circulo del grupo de las figuras.

Circle

Circulo

Directions: Draw your own circle in the blank space.

Instrucciones: Dibuje un circulo en el espacio.

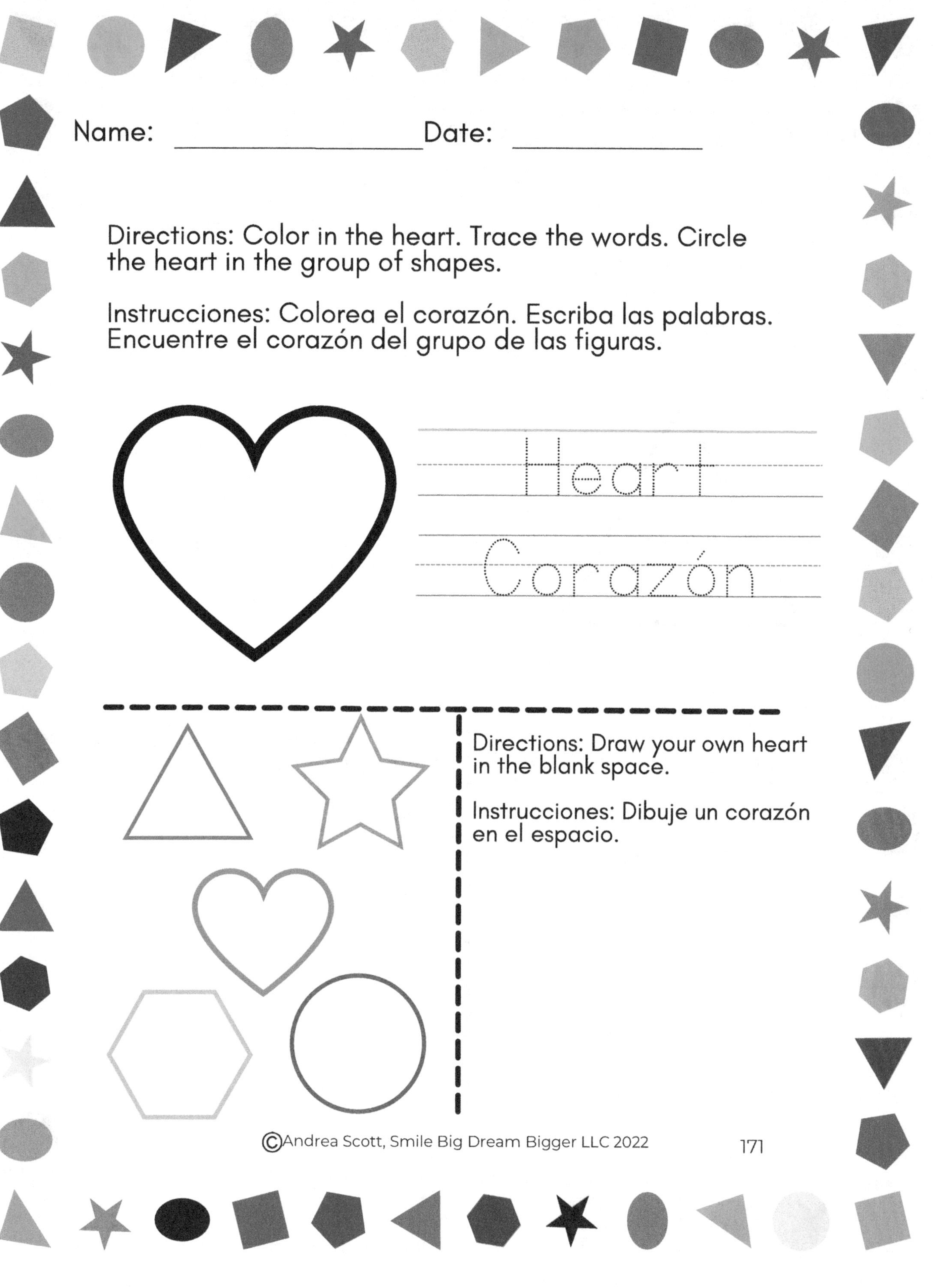
Name: Date:
Directions: Color in the heart. Trace the words. Circle the heart in the group of shapes.
Instrucciones: Colorea el corazón. Escriba las palabras. Encuentre el corazón del grupo de las figuras.
Heart
Corazón
Directions: Draw your own heart in the blank space.
Instrucciones: Dibuje un corazón en el espacio.

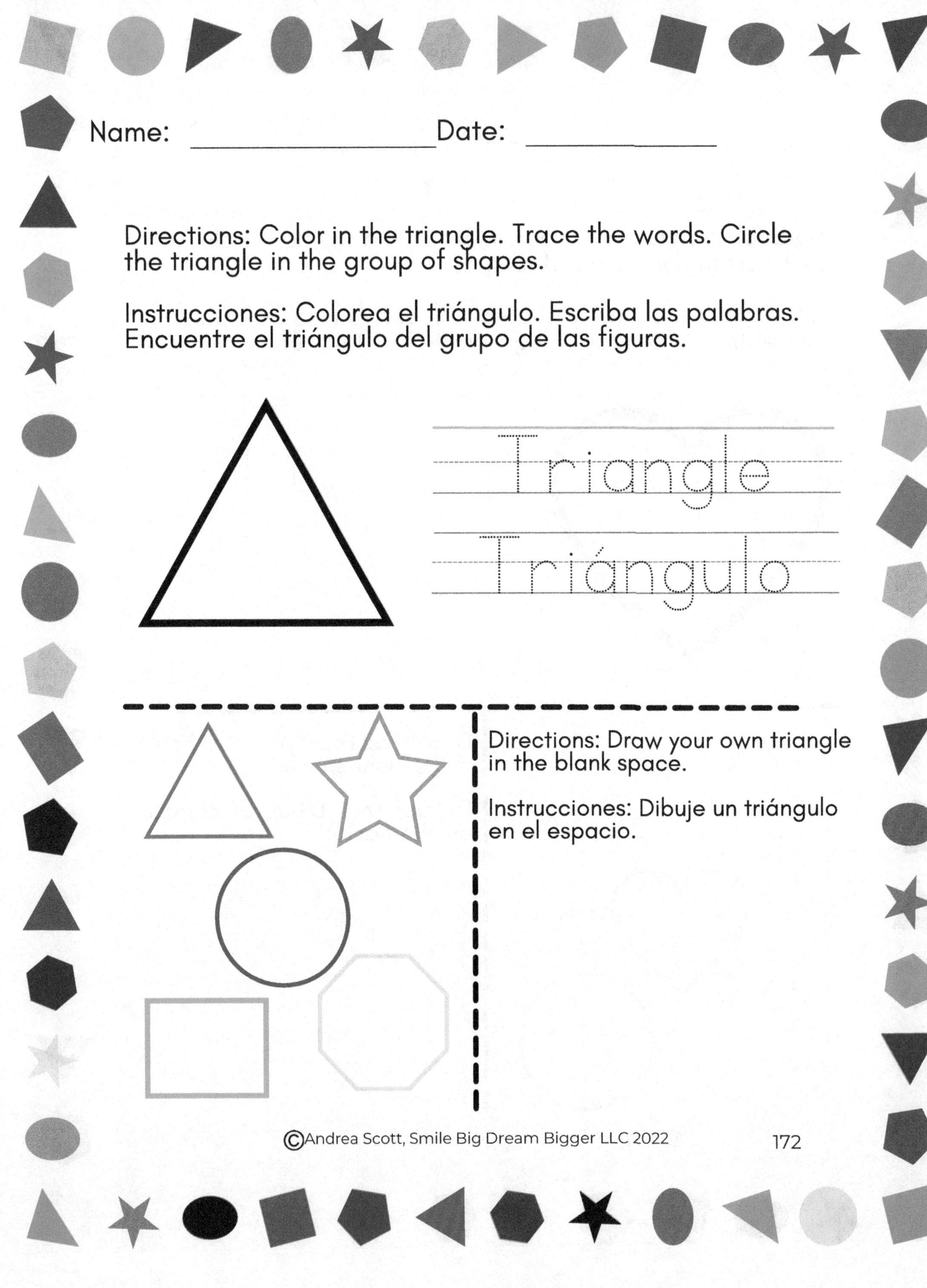

Name: ____________________Date: ______________

Directions: Color in the triangle. Trace the words. Circle the triangle in the group of shapes.

Instrucciones: Colorea el triángulo. Escriba las palabras. Encuentre el triángulo del grupo de las figuras.

Triangle

Triángulo

Directions: Draw your own triangle in the blank space.

Instrucciones: Dibuje un triángulo en el espacio.

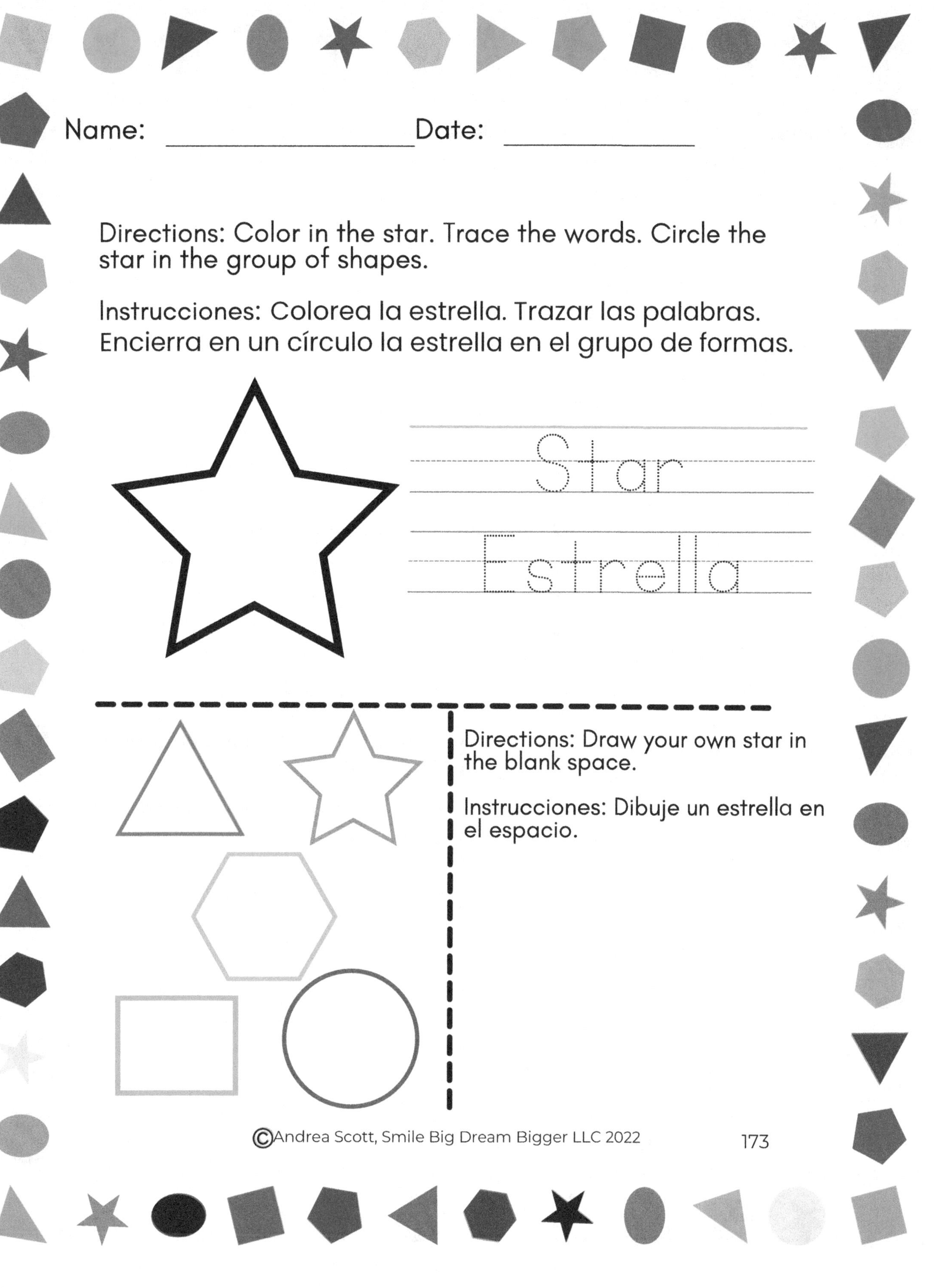

Name: ____________________ Date: ______________

Directions: Color in the star. Trace the words. Circle the star in the group of shapes.

Instrucciones: Colorea la estrella. Trazar las palabras. Encierra en un círculo la estrella en el grupo de formas.

Star
Estrella

Directions: Draw your own star in the blank space.

Instrucciones: Dibuje un estrella en el espacio.

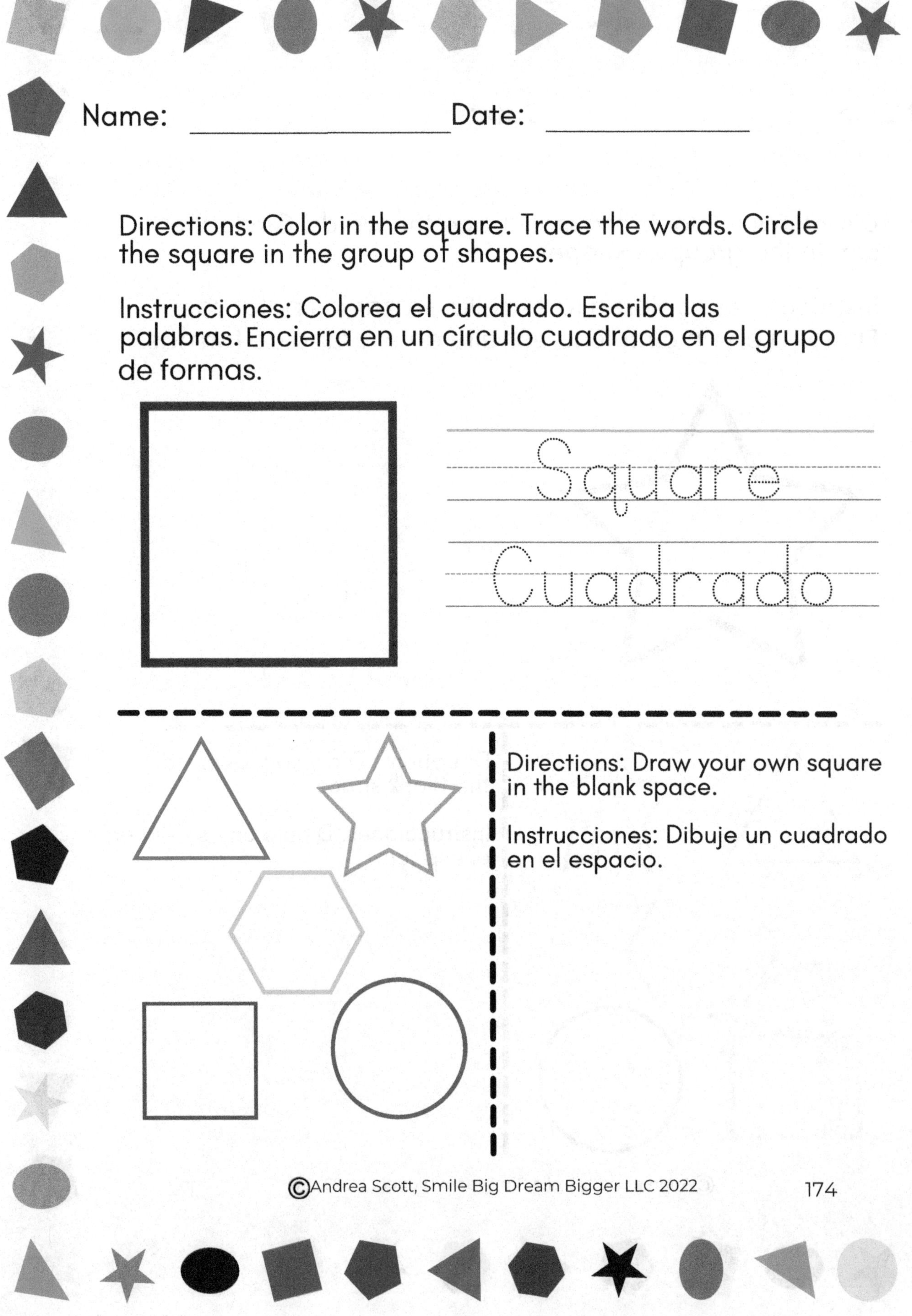

Name: ____________________ Date: ________________

Directions: Color in the square. Trace the words. Circle the square in the group of shapes.

Instrucciones: Colorea el cuadrado. Escriba las palabras. Encierra en un círculo cuadrado en el grupo de formas.

Square

Cuadrado

Directions: Draw your own square in the blank space.

Instrucciones: Dibuje un cuadrado en el espacio.

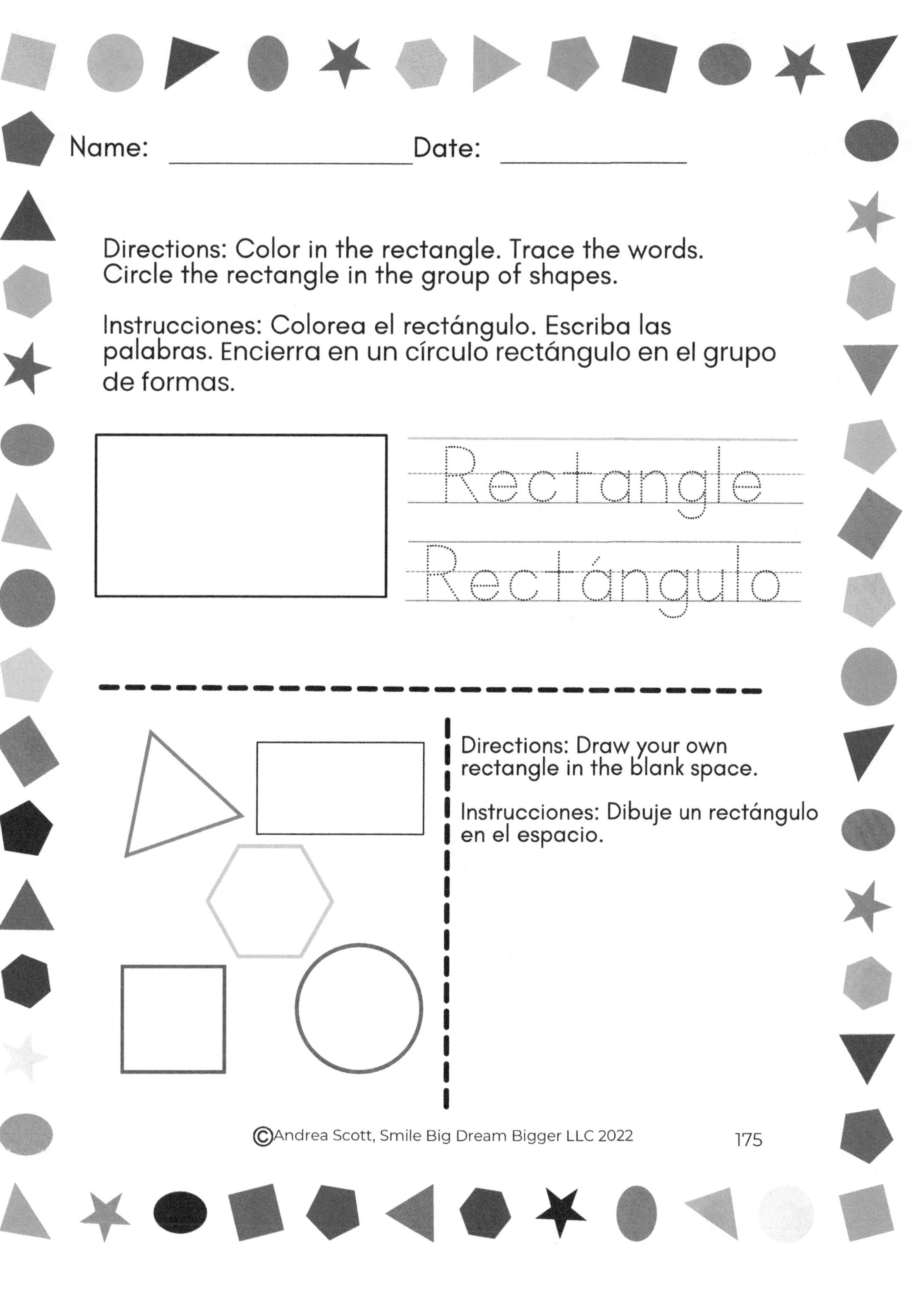

Name: Date:
Directions: Color in the rectangle. Trace the words.
Circle the rectangle in the group of shapes.
Instrucciones: Colorea el rectángulo. Escriba las
palabras. Encierra en un círculo rectángulo en el grupo
de formas.
Rectangle
Rectángulo
Directions: Draw your own
rectangle in the blank space.
Instrucciones: Dibuje un rectángulo
en el espacio.

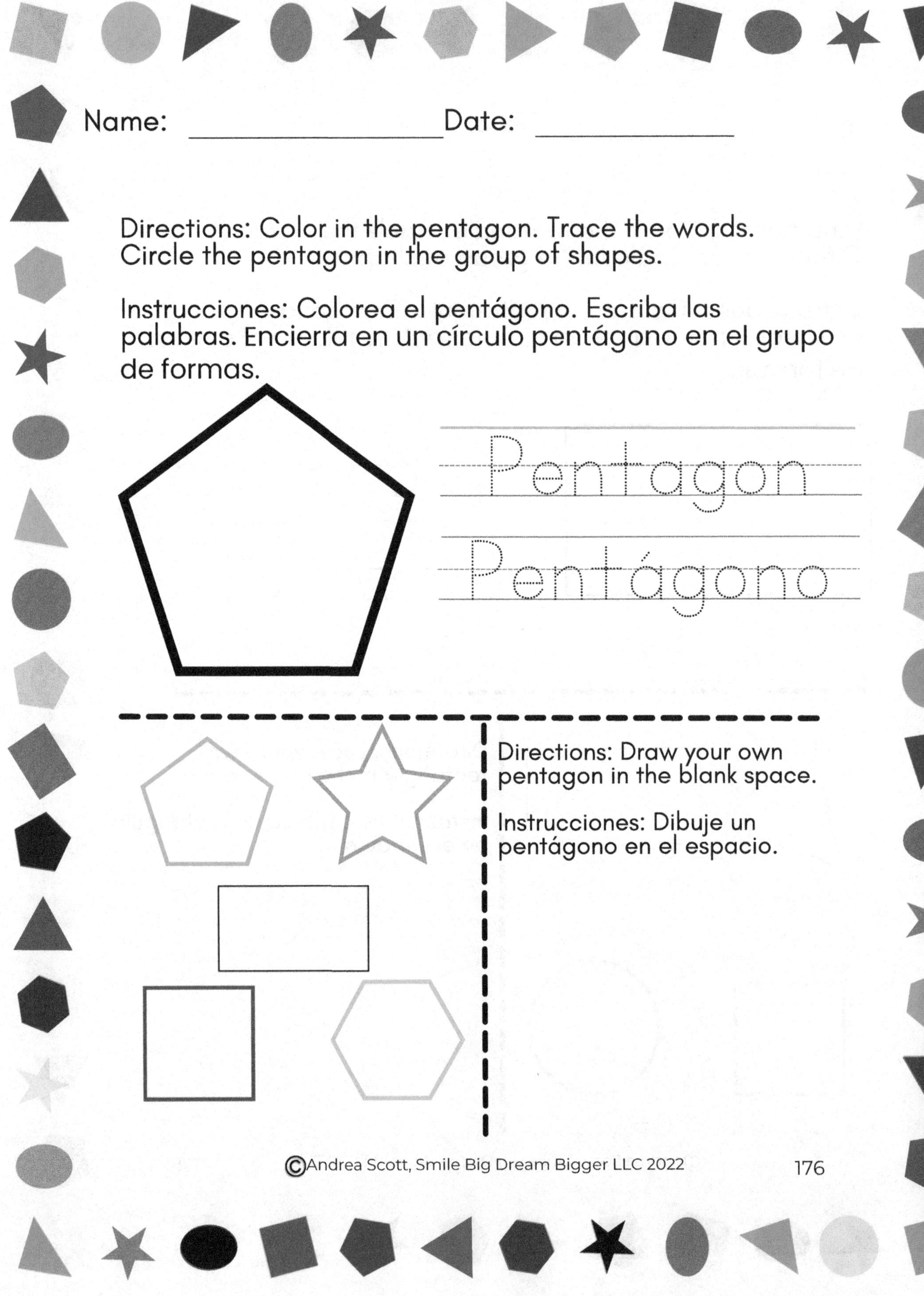

Name: ____________________ Date: ________________

Directions: Color in the pentagon. Trace the words. Circle the pentagon in the group of shapes.

Instrucciones: Colorea el pentágono. Escriba las palabras. Encierra en un círculo pentágono en el grupo de formas.

Directions: Draw your own pentagon in the blank space.

Instrucciones: Dibuje un pentágono en el espacio.

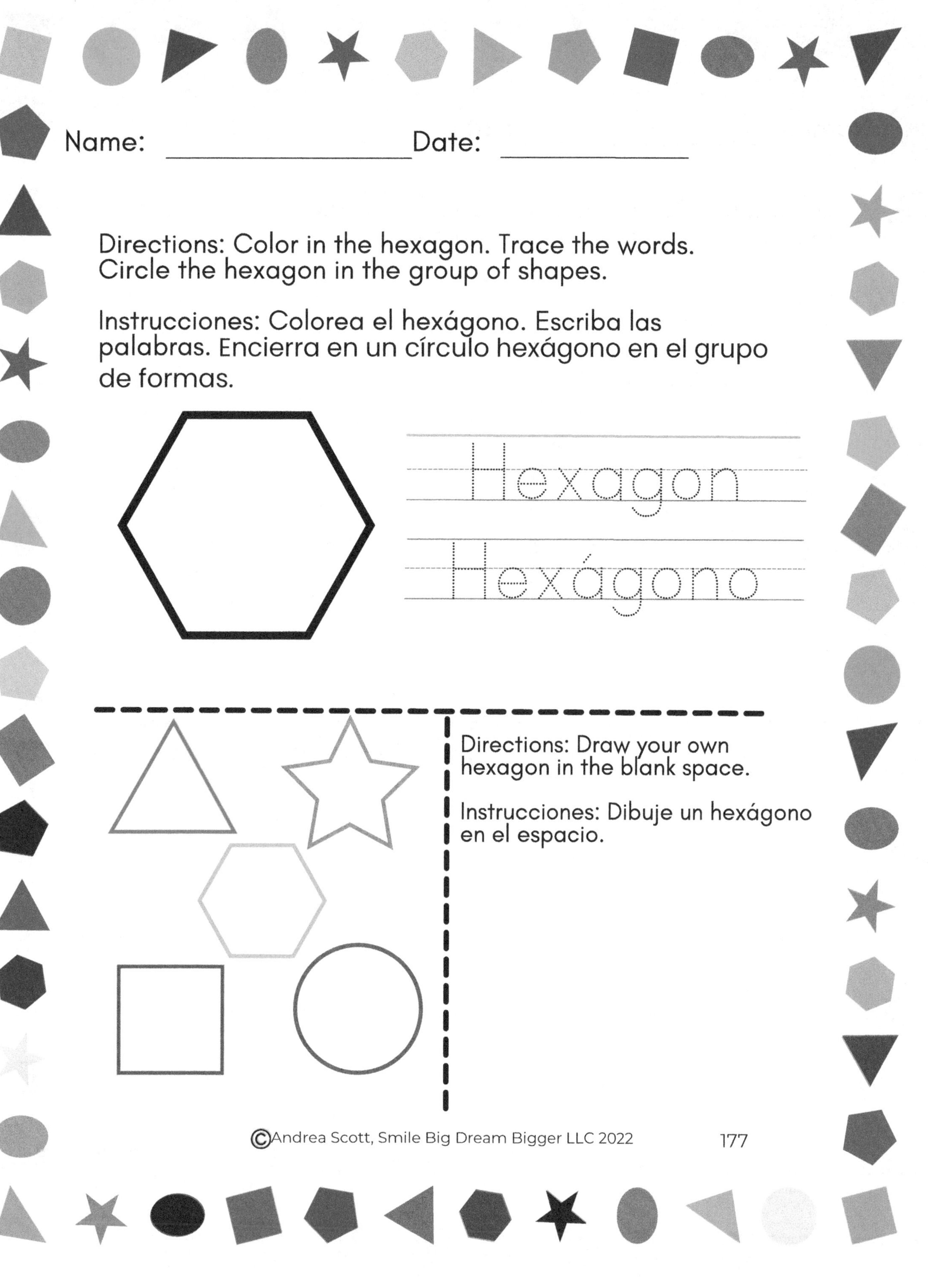

Name: Date:
Directions: Color in the hexagon. Trace the words.
Circle the hexagon in the group of shapes.
Instrucciones: Colorea el hexágono. Escriba las palabras. Encierra en un círculo hexágono en el grupo de formas.
Hexagon
Hexágono
Directions: Draw your own hexagon in the blank space.
Instrucciones: Dibuje un hexágono en el espacio.

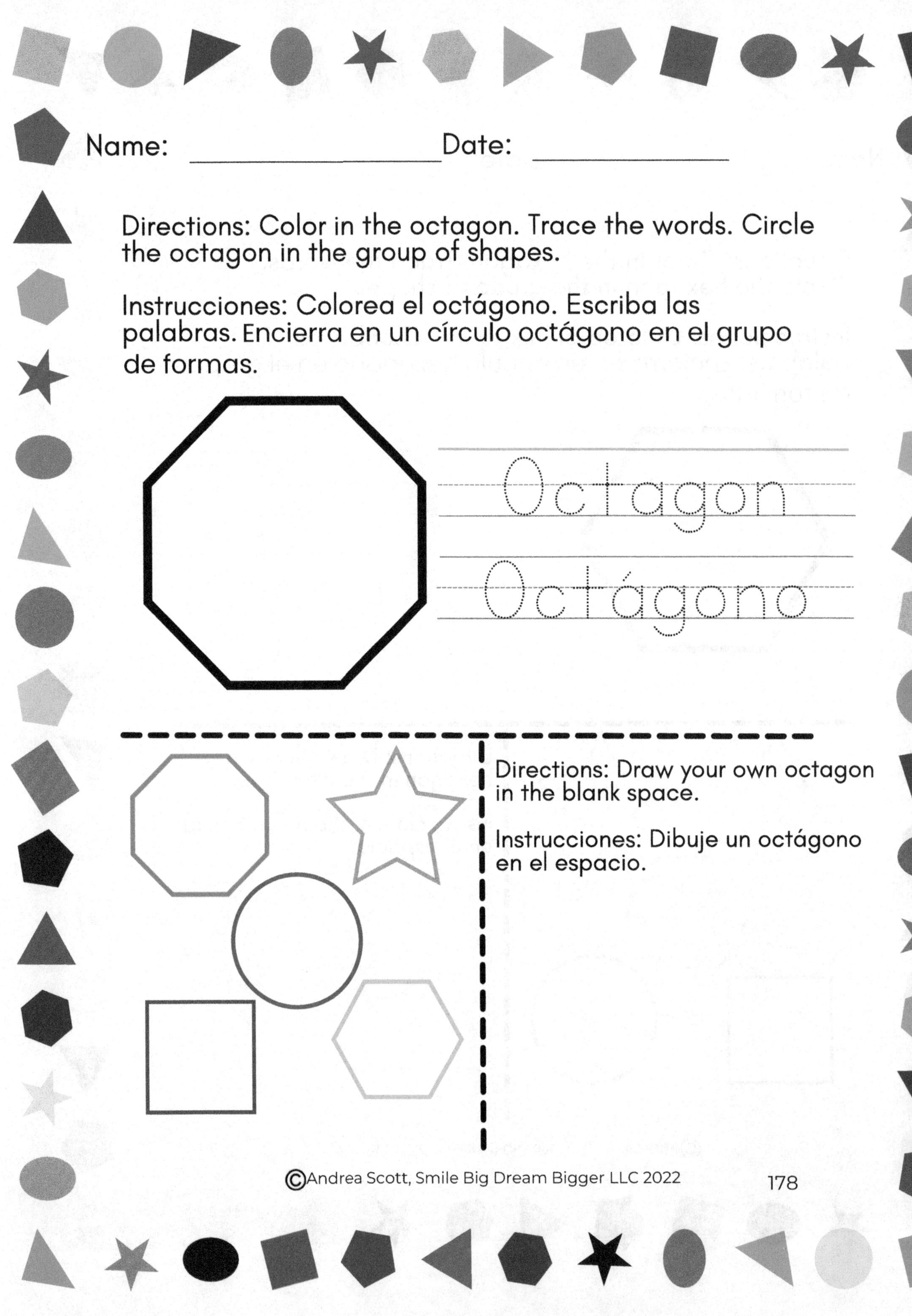

Name: ____________________Date: ______________

Directions: Color in the octagon. Trace the words. Circle the octagon in the group of shapes.

Instrucciones: Colorea el octágono. Escriba las palabras. Encierra en un círculo octágono en el grupo de formas.

Octagon

Octágono

Directions: Draw your own octagon in the blank space.

Instrucciones: Dibuje un octágono en el espacio.

Name: ____________________ Date: ______________

Shaping My Fro'

Directions: Count the shapes in the afro and place the number in the box. Color the shapes and afro when you are finished.

Instruccions: Cuenta las formas en el afro' y coloque el número en el cuadro. Colorea las formas y afro' cuando hayas terminado.

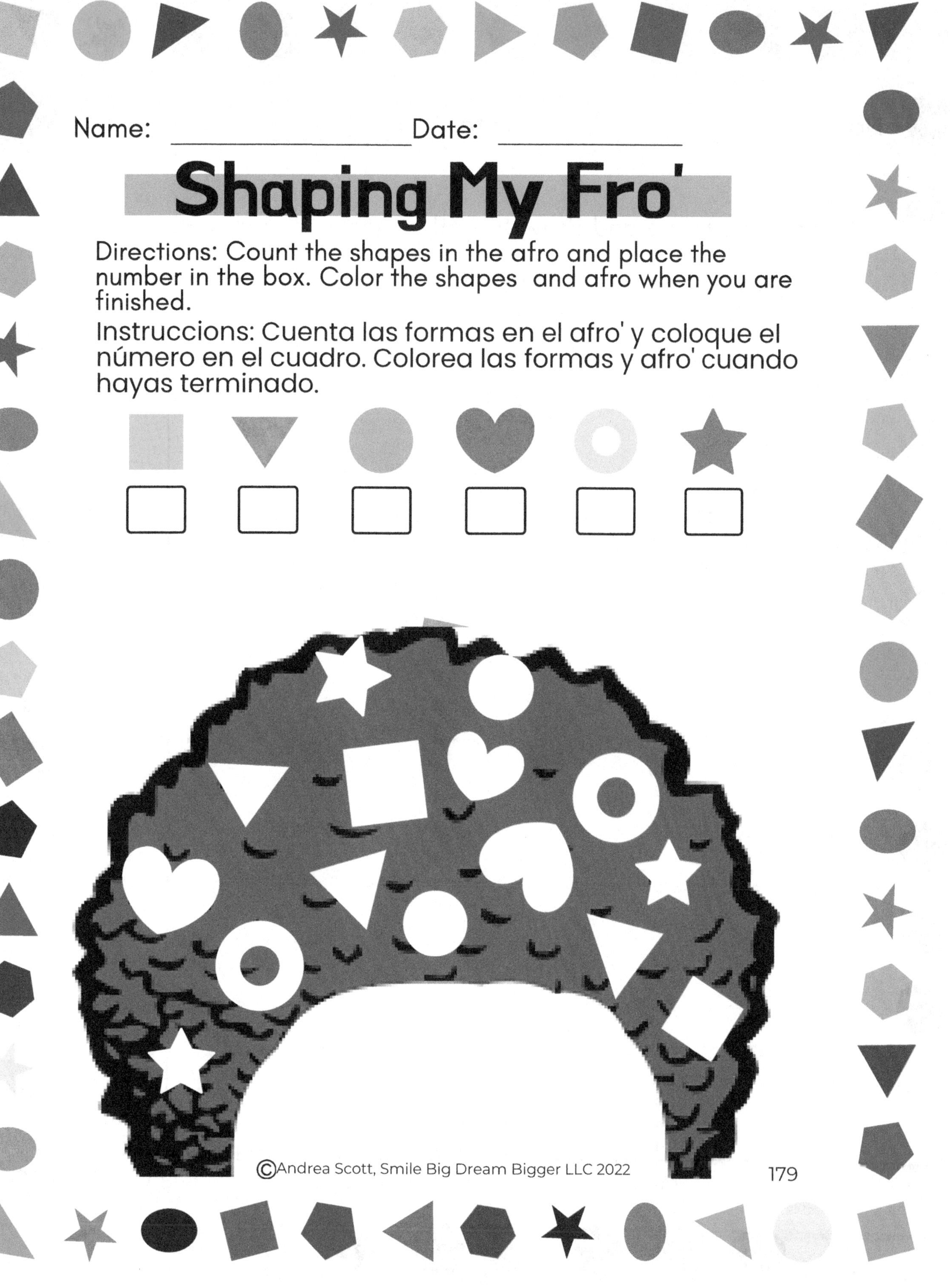

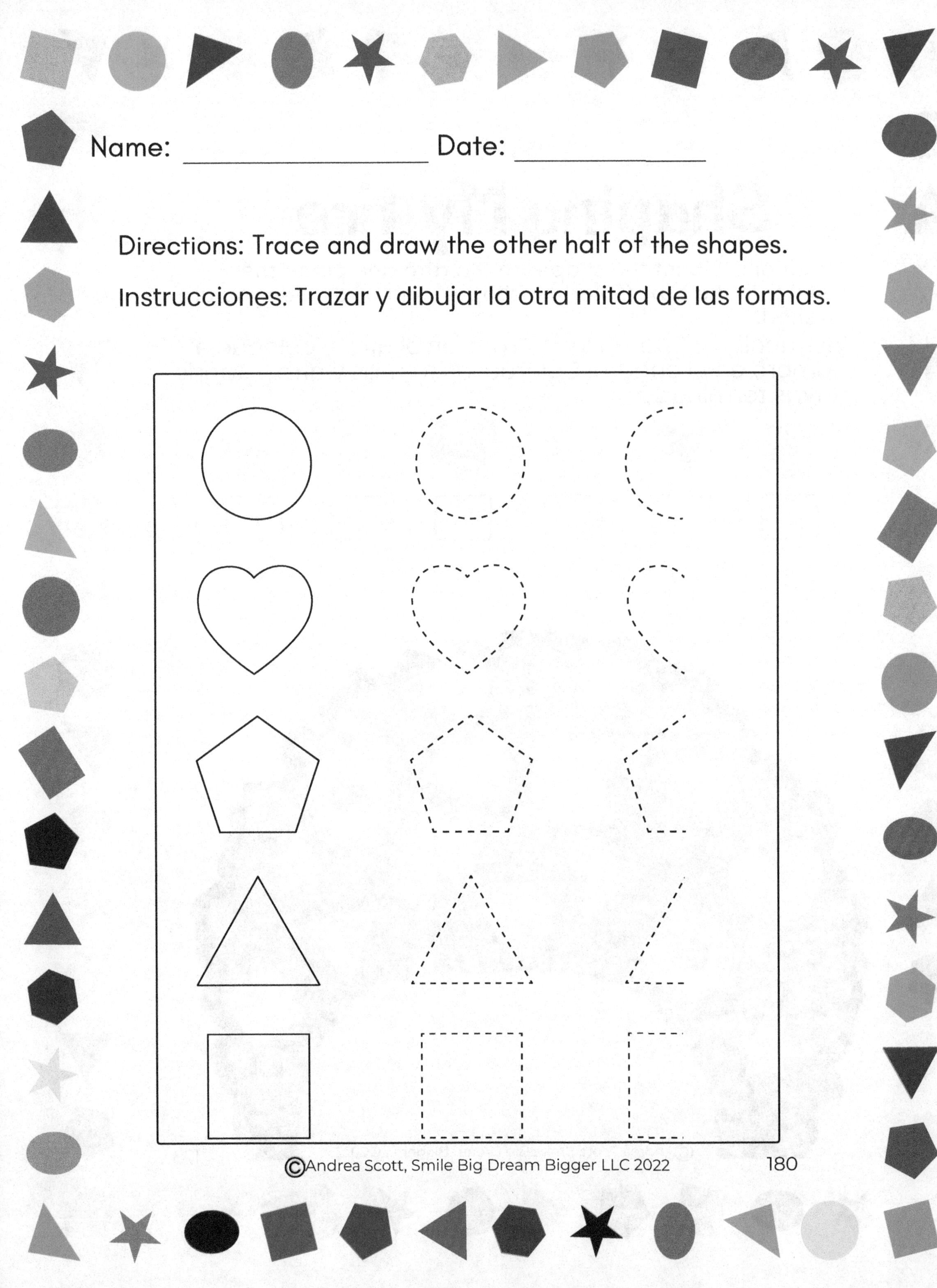

Name: _______________ Date: _______________

Directions: Trace and draw the other half of the shapes.

Instrucciones: Trazar y dibujar la otra mitad de las formas.

Name: ____________________ Date: ________________

Shapes/Las Figuras

LET'S DRAW AND COLOR!

Directions: Color the squares green, the circles yellow, and the triangles brown.

Instrucciones: Colorea los cuadros azules, los circulos amarillos, y los triángulos marrones.

Name: ______________________ Date: ________________

Patterns/Patrones

Directions: Select the shape the comes next in the sequence.
Instrucciones: Elige la forma siguiente en la secuencia.

Numbers/Los Números

Name: ______________________ Date: _______________

Directions/Instrucciones:

1. Trace the numbers/ Trazar el número

1	2	3	4	5
6	7	8	9	10
11	12	13	14	15
16	17	18	19	20

Name: ___________________________

Directions/Instrucciones:

1. Trace the numbers/ Trazar el número

Counting my Afro Picks

Name: ___________________________

Directions/Instrucciones:

1. Trace the numbers/ Trazar el número

Counting my Afro Picks

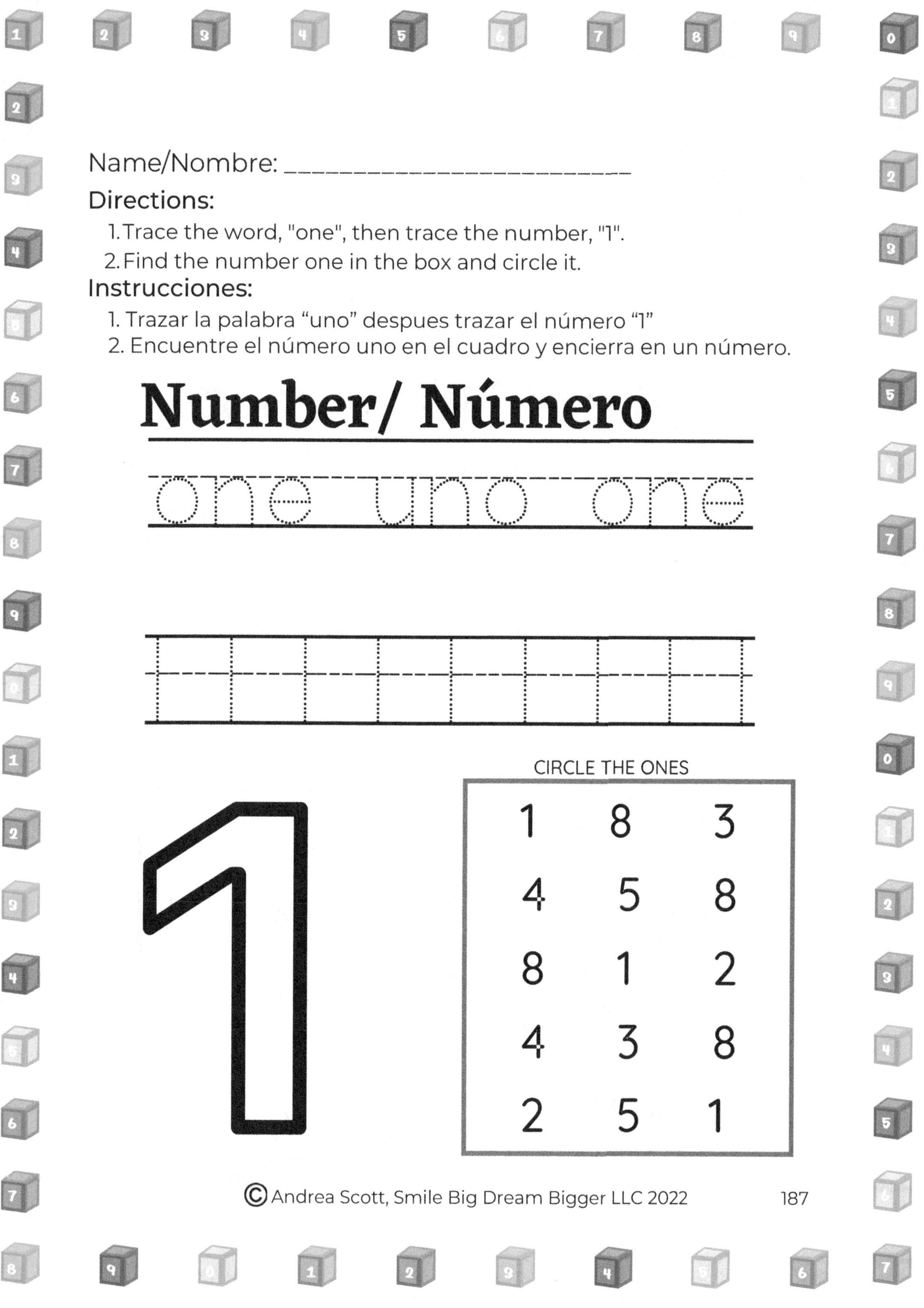

Name/Nombre: ___________________________

Directions:

1. Trace the word, "one", then trace the number, "1".
2. Find the number one in the box and circle it.

Instrucciones:

1. Trazar la palabra “uno” despues trazar el número “1”
2. Encuentre el número uno en el cuadro y encierra en un número.

Number/ Número

one uno one

1

CIRCLE THE ONES

1	8	3
4	5	8
8	1	2
4	3	8
2	5	1

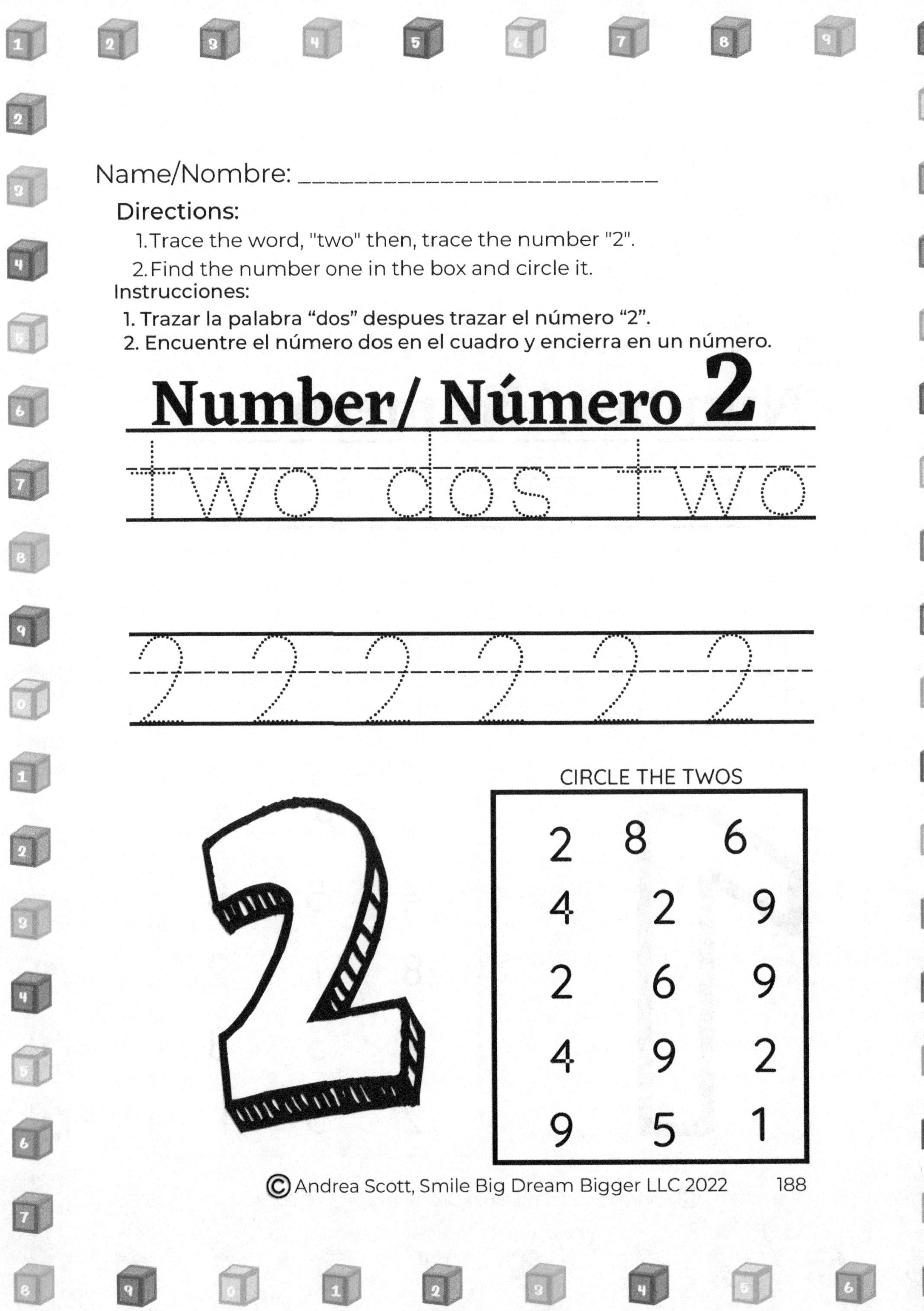

Name/Nombre: ___________________________

Directions:

1. Trace the word, "two" then, trace the number "2".
2. Find the number one in the box and circle it.

Instrucciones:

1. Trazar la palabra “dos” despues trazar el número “2”.
2. Encuentre el número dos en el cuadro y encierra en un número.

Number/ Número 2

two dos two

2 2 2 2 2 2

CIRCLE THE TWOS

2	8	6
4	2	9
2	6	9
4	9	2
9	5	1

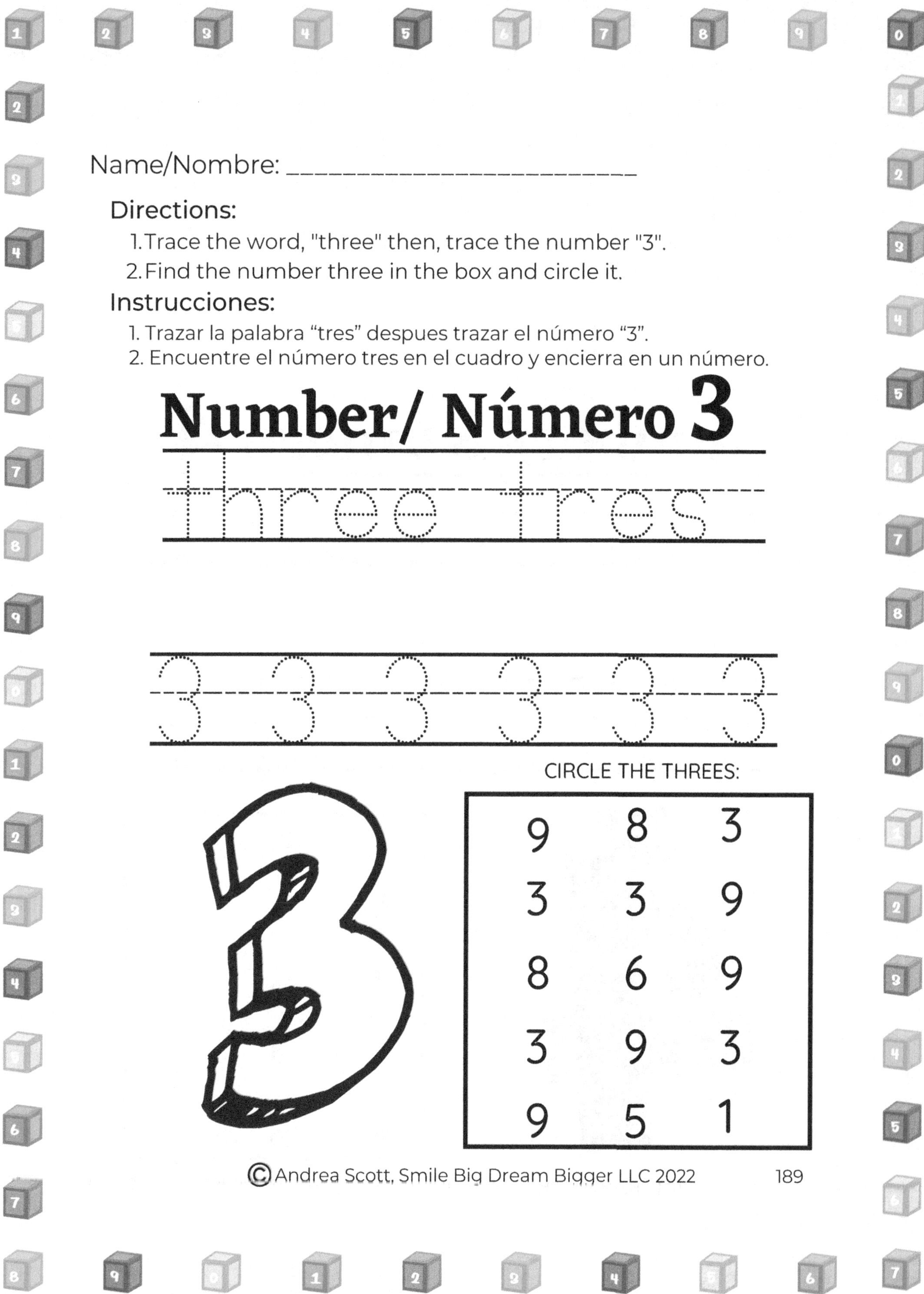

Name/Nombre: ___________________________

Directions:

1. Trace the word, "three" then, trace the number "3".
2. Find the number three in the box and circle it.

Instrucciones:

1. Trazar la palabra “tres” despues trazar el número “3”.
2. Encuentre el número tres en el cuadro y encierra en un número.

Number/ Número 3

three tres

3 3 3 3 3 3

CIRCLE THE THREES:

9	8	3
3	3	9
8	6	9
3	9	3
9	5	1

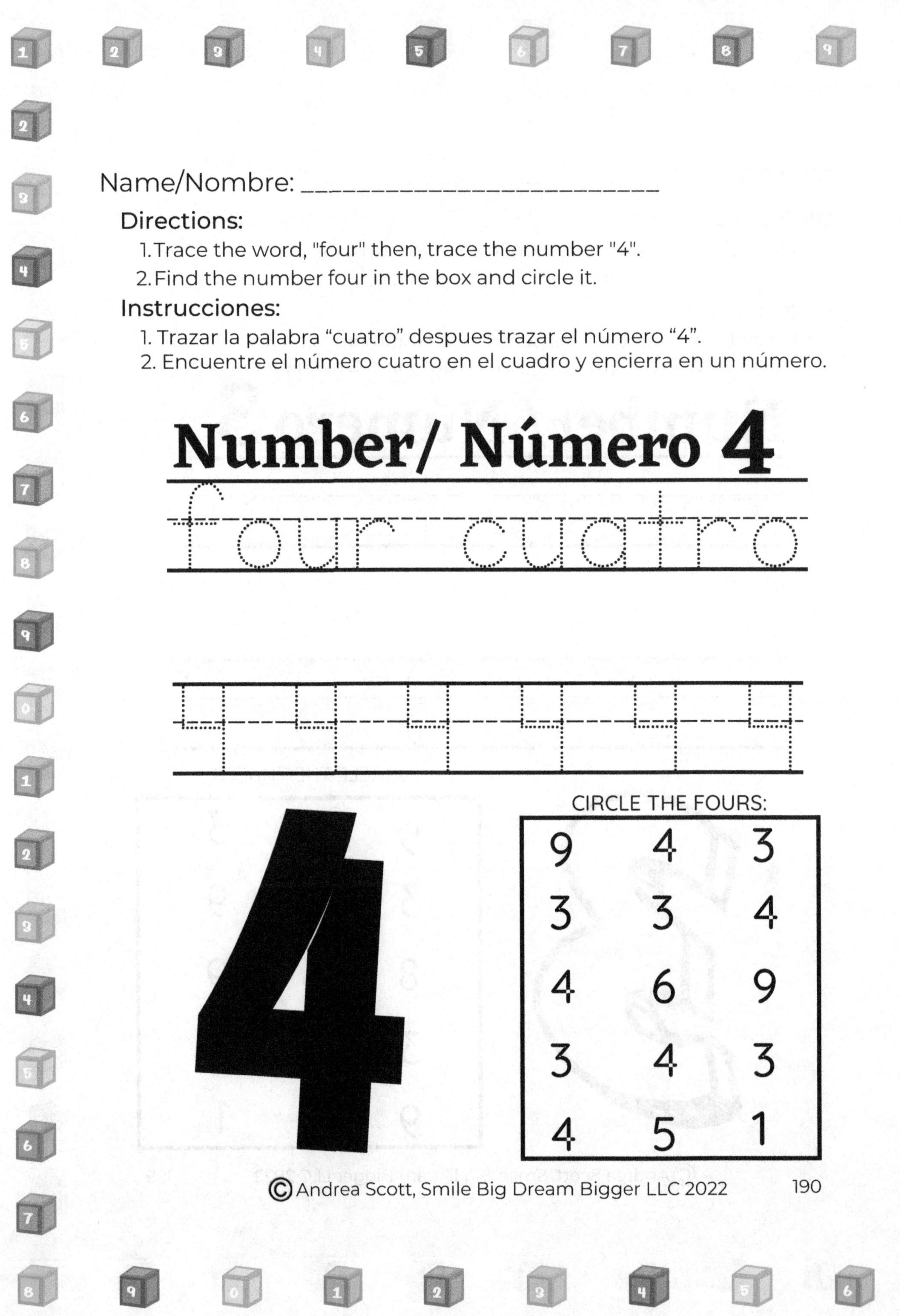

Name/Nombre: ___________________________

Directions:

1. Trace the word, "four" then, trace the number "4".
2. Find the number four in the box and circle it.

Instrucciones:

1. Trazar la palabra “cuatro” despues trazar el número “4”.
2. Encuentre el número cuatro en el cuadro y encierra en un número.

Number/ Número 4

four cuatro

CIRCLE THE FOURS:

9	4	3
3	3	4
4	6	9
3	4	3
4	5	1

Name/Nombre: ___________________________

Directions:

1. Trace the word, "five" then, trace the number "5".
2. Find the number five in the box and circle it.

Instrucciones:

1. Trazar la palabra “cinco” despues trazar el número “5”.
2. Encuentre el número cinco en el cuadro y encierra en un número.

Number/ Número 5

five cinco five

5 5 5 5 5 5

5

CIRCLE THE FIVES:

5	4	3
3	5	4
4	6	5
3	4	3
5	5	1

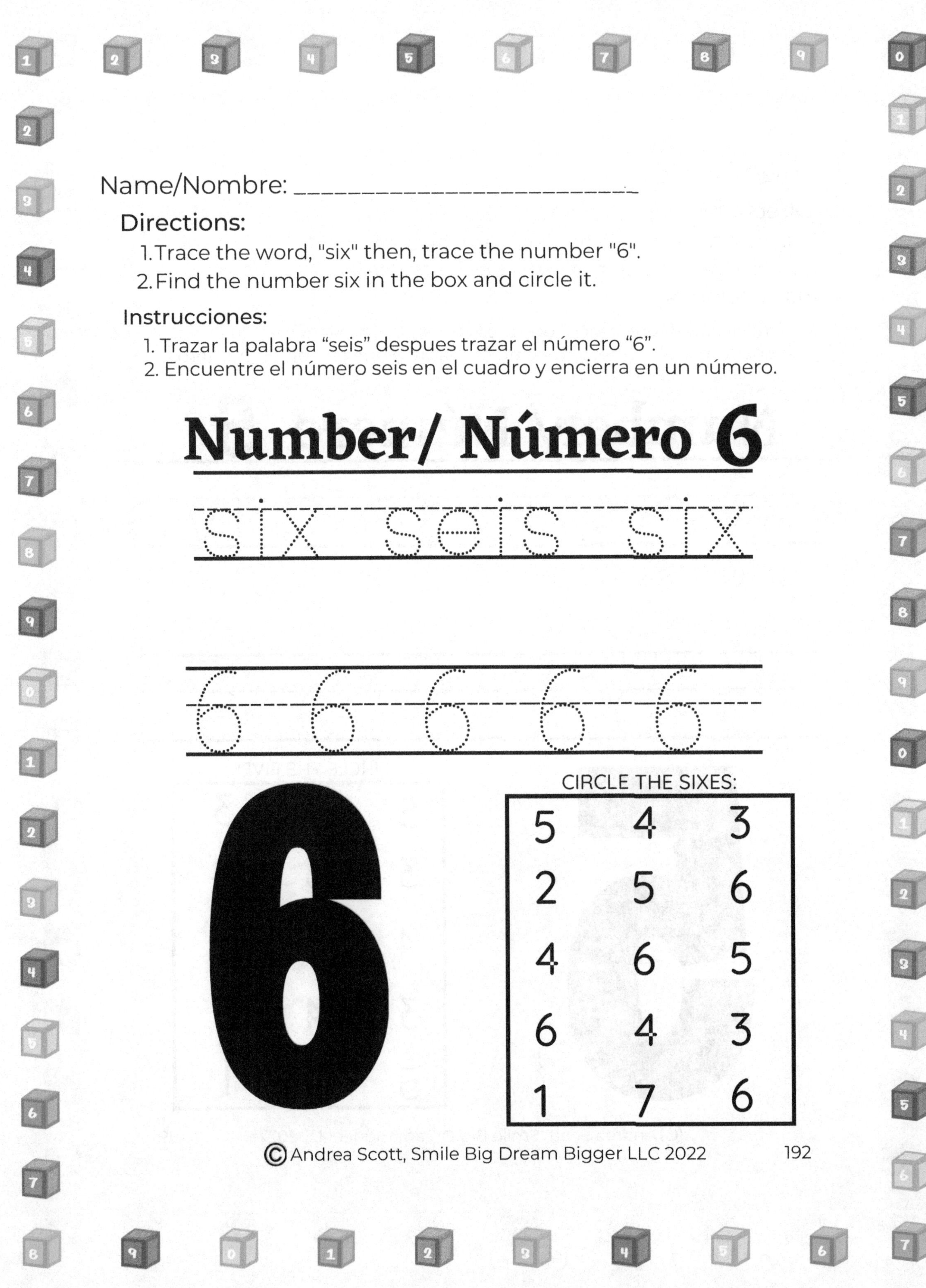

Name/Nombre: ___________________________

Directions:

1. Trace the word, "six" then, trace the number "6".
2. Find the number six in the box and circle it.

Instrucciones:

1. Trazar la palabra “seis” despues trazar el número “6”.
2. Encuentre el número seis en el cuadro y encierra en un número.

Number/ Número 6

six seis six

6 6 6 6 6

6

CIRCLE THE SIXES:

5	4	3
2	5	6
4	6	5
6	4	3
1	7	6

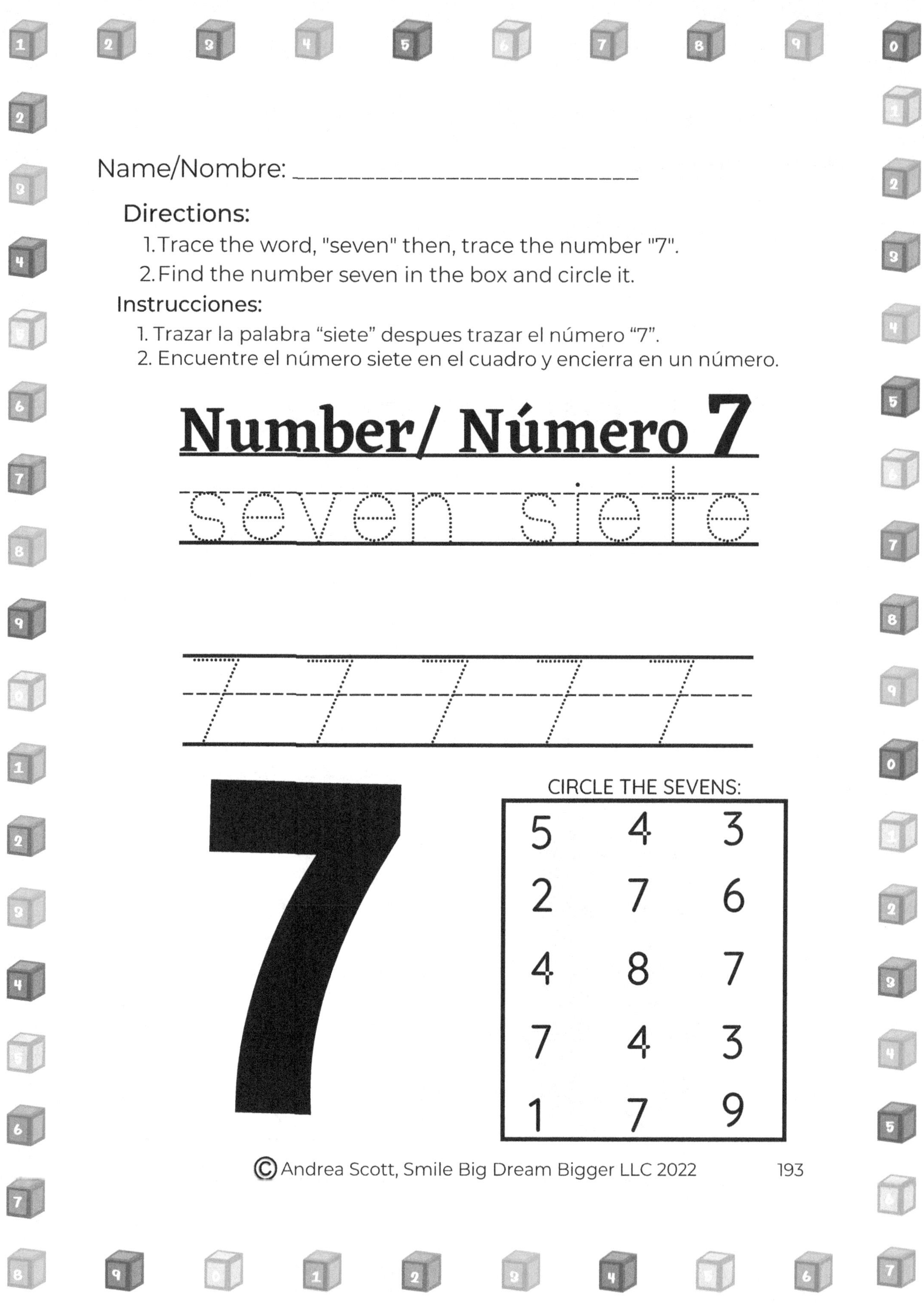

Name/Nombre: ____________________________

Directions:

1. Trace the word, "seven" then, trace the number "7".
2. Find the number seven in the box and circle it.

Instrucciones:

1. Trazar la palabra "siete" despues trazar el número "7".
2. Encuentre el número siete en el cuadro y encierra en un número.

Number/ Número 7

seven siete

7 7 7 7 7

7

CIRCLE THE SEVENS:

5	4	3
2	7	6
4	8	7
7	4	3
1	7	9

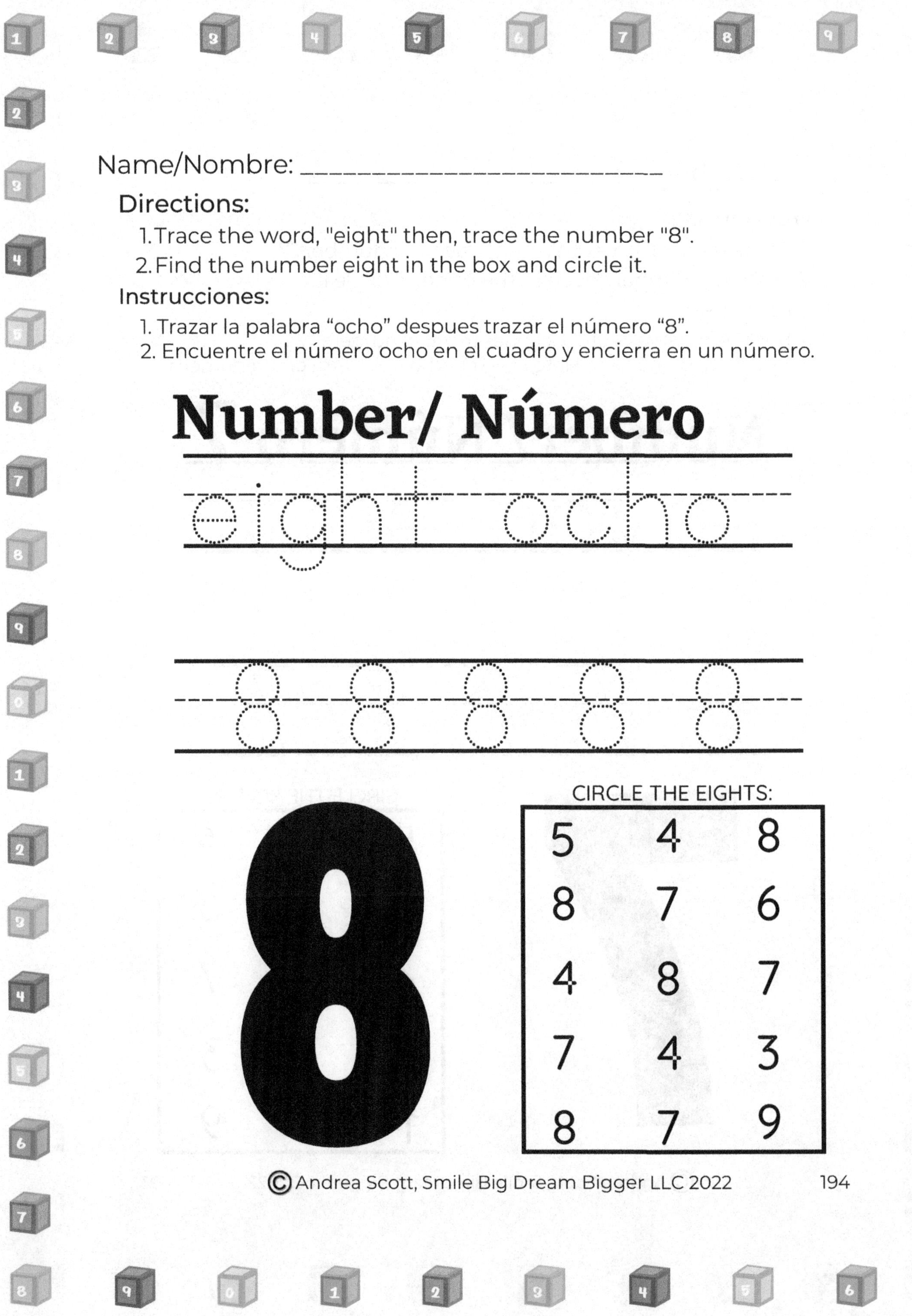

Name/Nombre: ___________________________

Directions:

1. Trace the word, "eight" then, trace the number "8".
2. Find the number eight in the box and circle it.

Instrucciones:

1. Trazar la palabra "ocho" despues trazar el número "8".
2. Encuentre el número ocho en el cuadro y encierra en un número.

Number/ Número

eight ocho

8 8 8 8 8

CIRCLE THE EIGHTS:

5	4	8
8	7	6
4	8	7
7	4	3
8	7	9

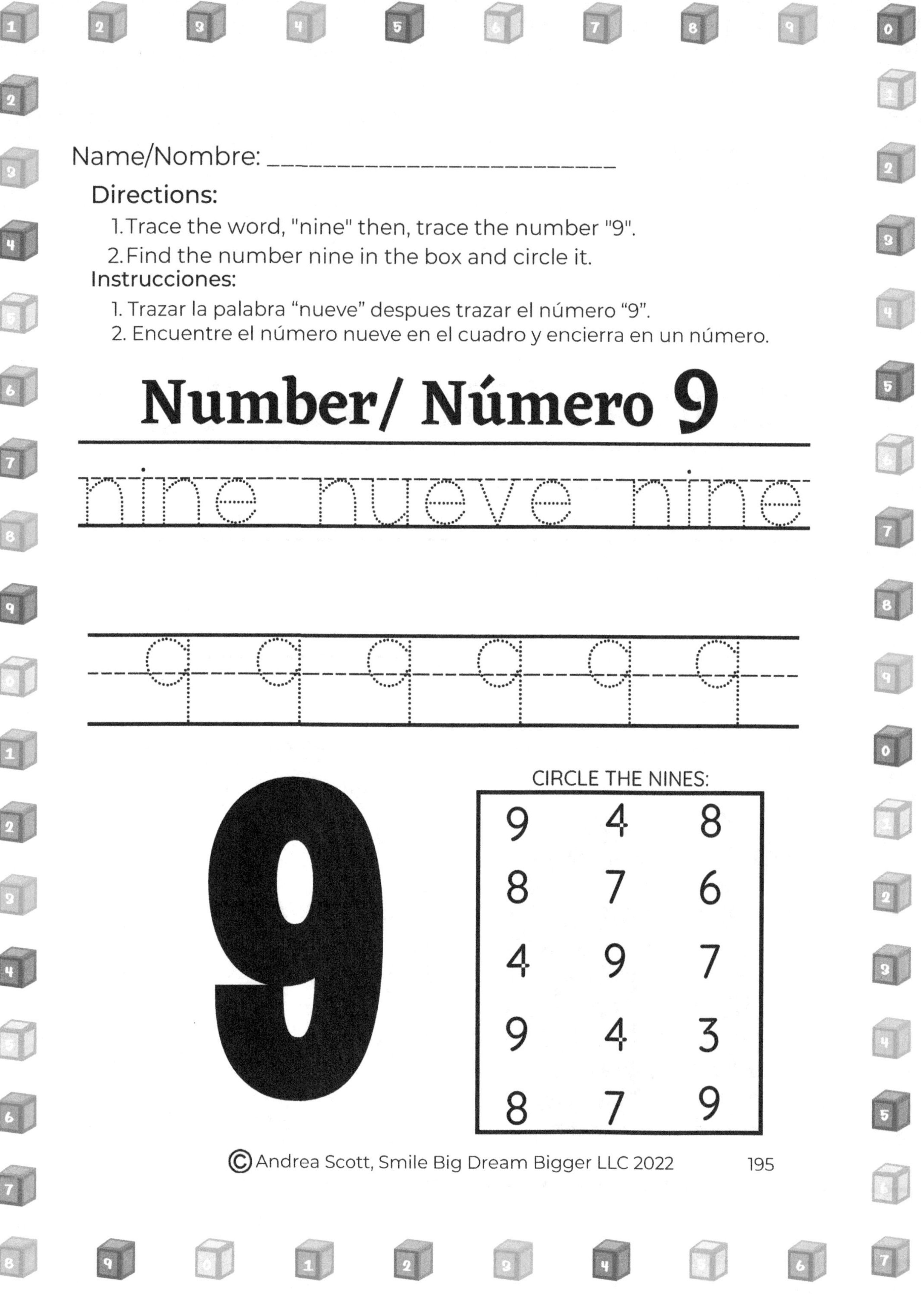

Name/Nombre: ___________________________

Directions:

1. Trace the word, "nine" then, trace the number "9".
2. Find the number nine in the box and circle it.

Instrucciones:

1. Trazar la palabra “nueve” despues trazar el número “9”.
2. Encuentre el número nueve en el cuadro y encierra en un número.

Number/ Número 9

nine nueve nine

9 9 9 9 9 9

9

CIRCLE THE NINES:

9	4	8
8	7	6
4	9	7
9	4	3
8	7	9

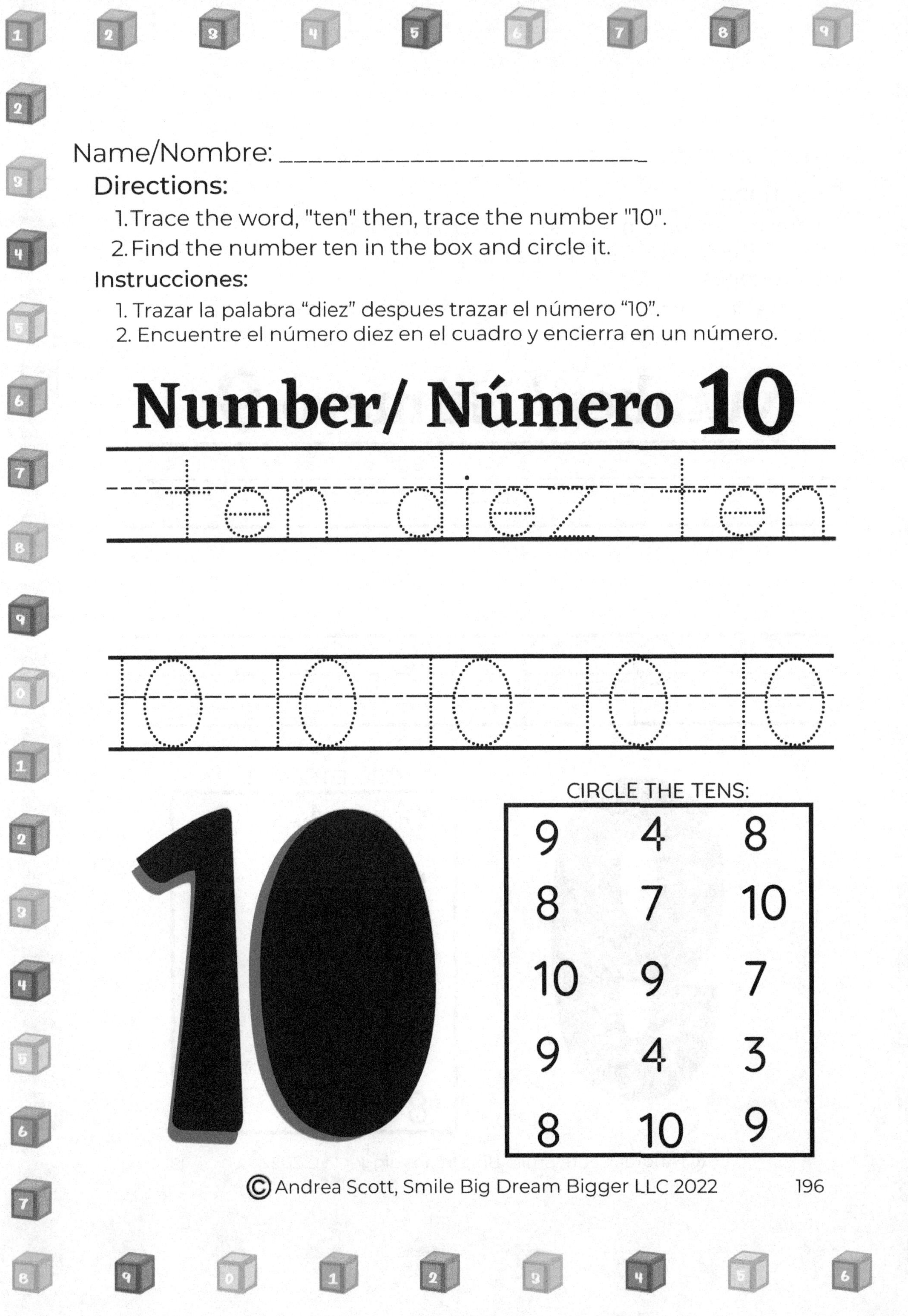

Name/Nombre: ___________________________

Directions:

1. Trace the word, "ten" then, trace the number "10".
2. Find the number ten in the box and circle it.

Instrucciones:

1. Trazar la palabra "diez" despues trazar el número "10".
2. Encuentre el número diez en el cuadro y encierra en un número.

Number/ Número 10

ten diez ten

10 10 10 10 10

CIRCLE THE TENS:

9	4	8
8	7	10
10	9	7
9	4	3
8	10	9

Name/Nombre: ___________________________
Directions:
1.Count the images and trace the number.
Instrucciones:
Cuenta las imágenes y traza el número
1 1 1 1 1 1
2 2 2 2 2
3 3 3 3 3
4 4 4 4 4
5 5 5 5 5

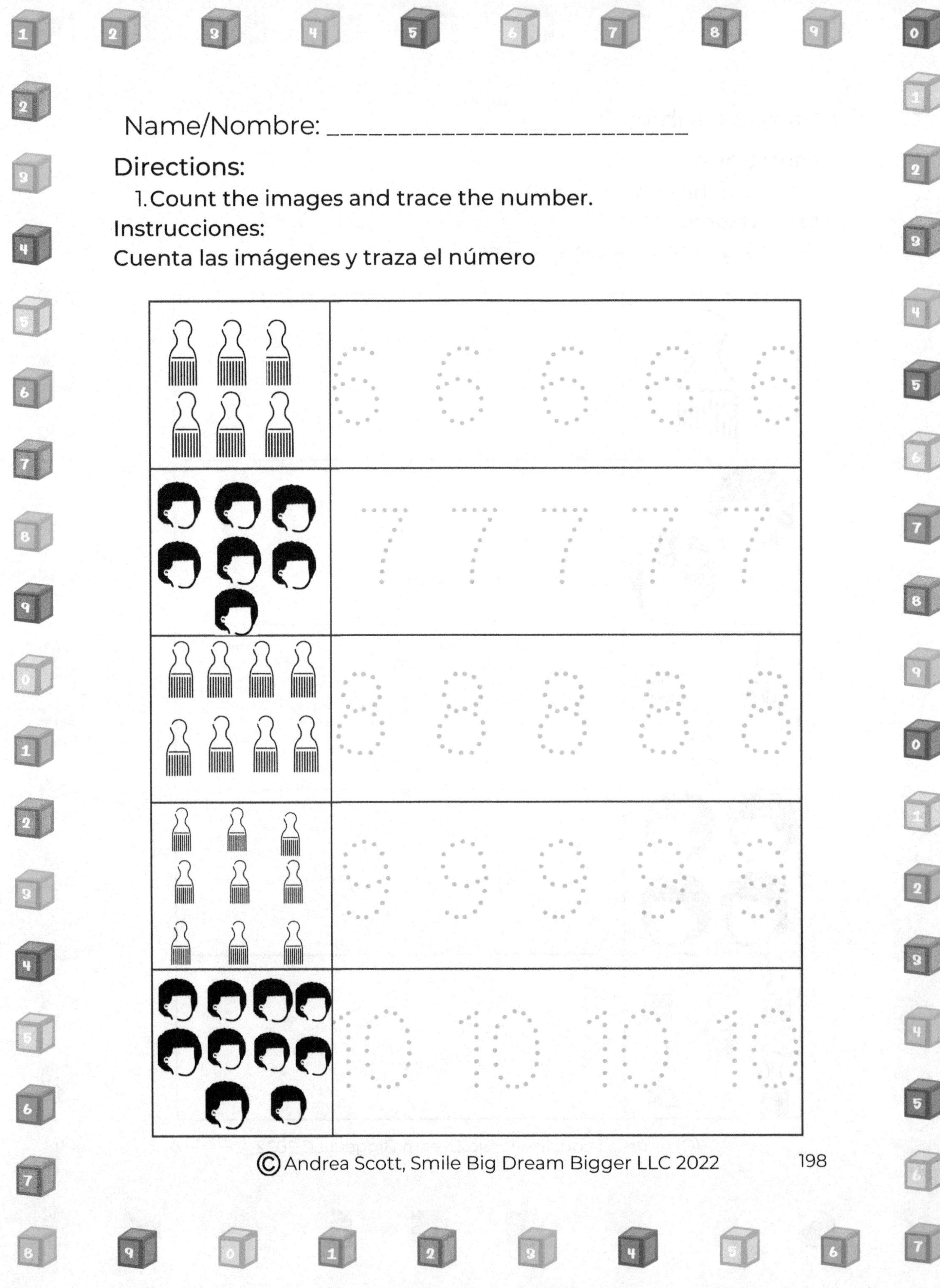

Name/Nombre: ______________________________

Directions:

1. Count the images and trace the number.

Instrucciones:

Cuenta las imágenes y traza el número

	6 6 6 6 6
	7 7 7 7 7
	8 8 8 8 8
	9 9 9 9 9
	10 10 10 10

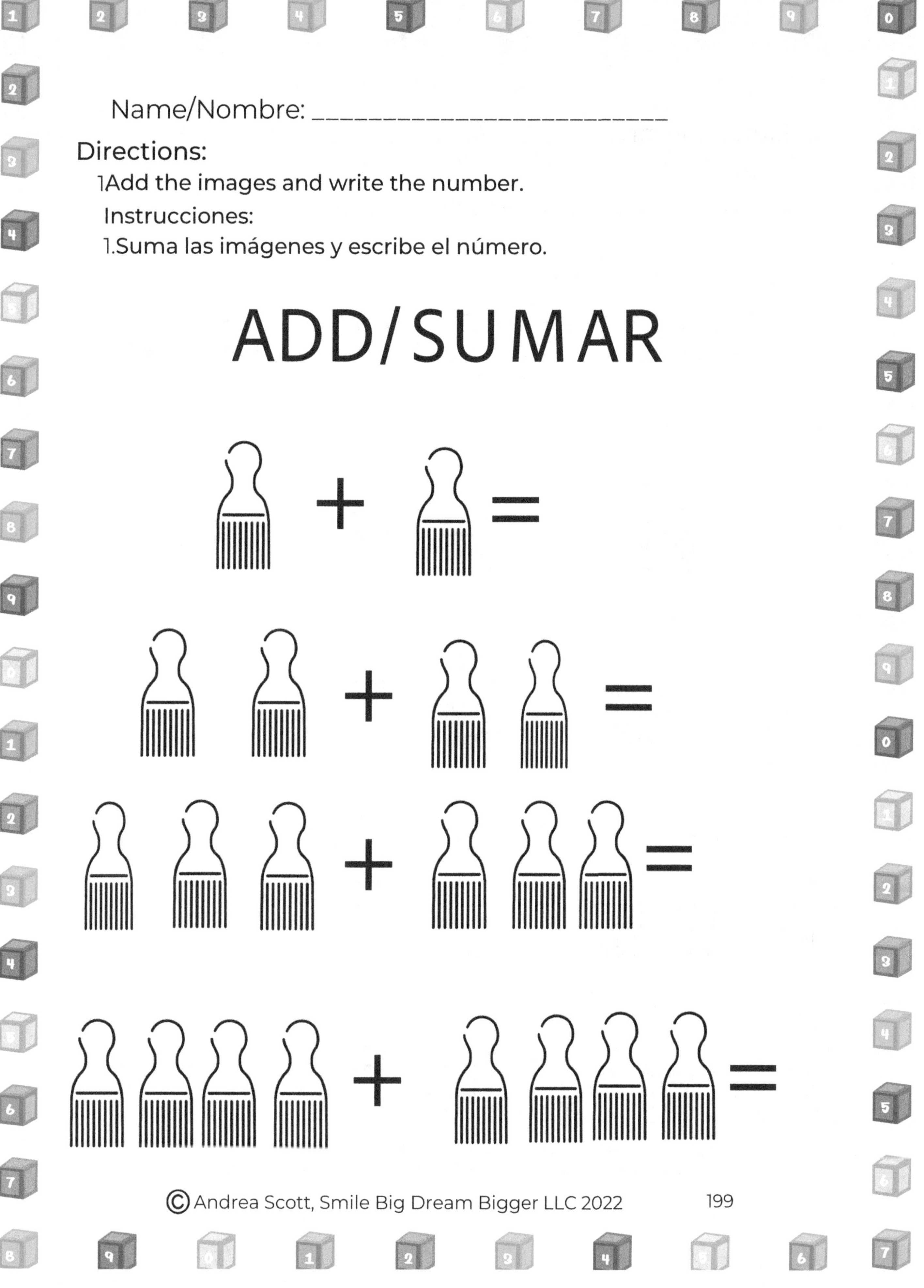

Name/Nombre: ___________________________

Directions:

1Add the images and write the number.

Instrucciones:

1.Suma las imágenes y escribe el número.

ADD/SUMAR

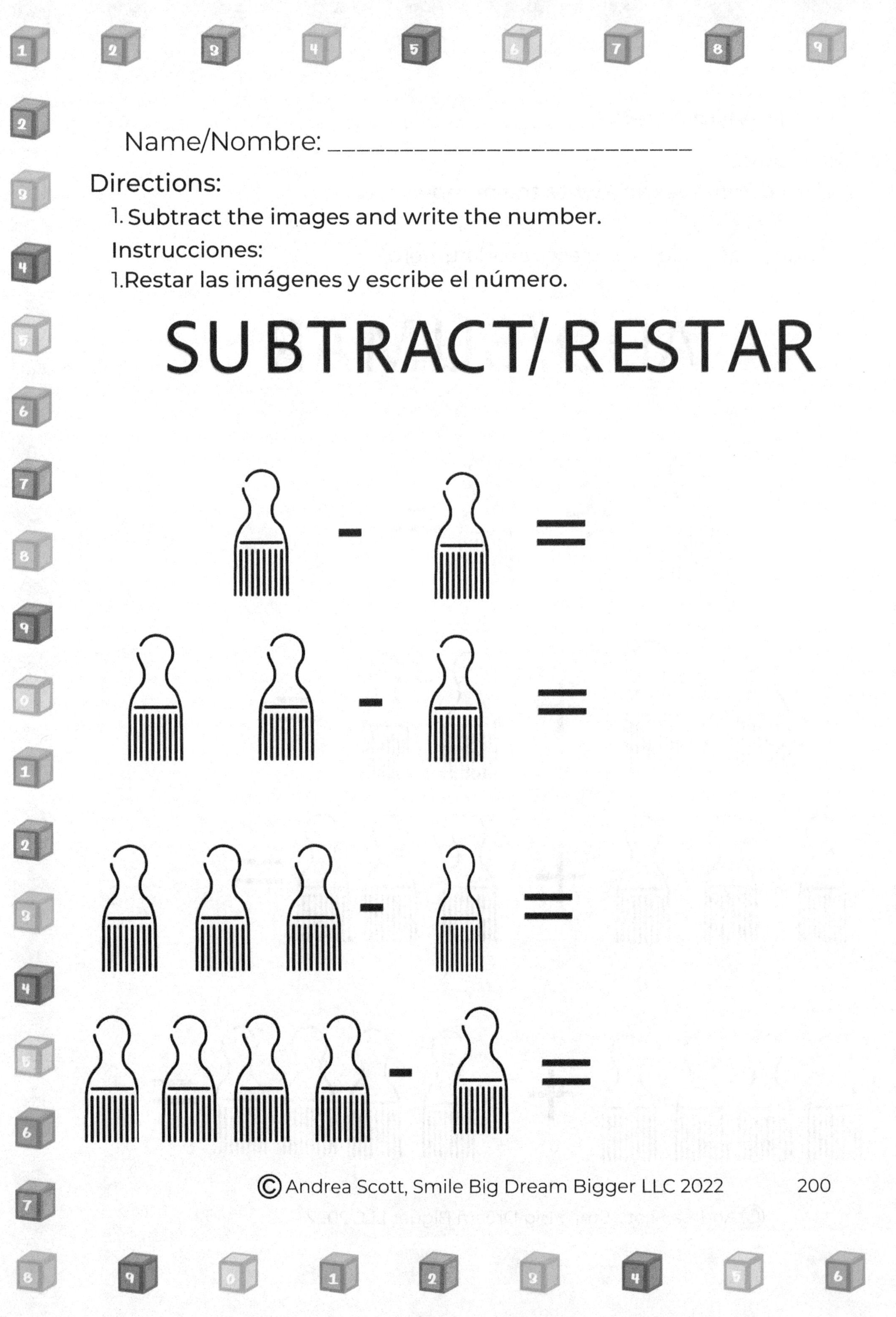

Name/Nombre: ____________________________

Directions:

1. Subtract the images and write the number.

Instrucciones:

1. Restar las imágenes y escribe el número.

SUBTRACT/ RESTAR

Made in the USA
Columbia, SC
16 August 2024

40059986R10111